AUTISM
THE WAY FORWARD

AUTISM
THE WAY FORWARD
A Self-Help Guide to Teaching
Children on the Autistic Spectrum

Stephanie Louise

Routledge
Taylor & Francis Group

LONDON AND NEW YORK

First published 2008 by Karnac Books Ltd.

Published 2018 by Routledge
2 Park Square, Milton Park, Abingdon, Oxon OX14 4RN
711 Third Avenue, New York, NY 10017, USA

Routledge is an imprint of the Taylor & Francis Group, an informa business

British Library Cataloguing in Publication Data

A C.I.P. for this book is available from the British Library

ISBN 9781855755987 (pbk)

Designed, typeset and produced by
Florence Production Ltd, Stoodleigh, Devon
www.florenceproduction.co.uk

Contents

ABOUT THE AUTHOR

Stephanie Louise is a communication specialist with a two-year under-graduate training in psychology. She has also trained at post-graduate level in psychological assessment and, as an undergraduate, with the English National Opera in music, art and dance therapy. In addition to her study of the "full communication" and Lovaas methods at Brunel University, she has developed an expertise in Applied Behaviour Analysis (ABA), Verbal Behaviour (VB) and child counselling.

PREFACE

This book was written in response to all those families who, due to lack of funding, were unable to access these means of intervention.

The book is written as though it were a therapy session, with would-be problems dealt with as they arise. As someone who saw, time after time, the impasse whenever the emotional realm was approached through the means of behavioural intervention, I decided to acquire the necessary training in order to help me to understand this aspect of the work better, and to enable me to implement this as much as possible into the therapeutic process.

After reading extensively into this subject I began to apply a different mindset to my work and thus began a marvellous journey into the world of autism. My accustomed way of looking at the child's behaviour no longer served me, I started to see and think differently, and so the children began to open up to me on a different level. As for the results, these were self-evident. As I discarded my cold, unresponsive training in behaviourism and began doing what worked, rather than what I was told, I found the children more responsive, I began to see them from a new perspective, and at times they appeared to step out of their autism, and connect with me on a deeper level.

The journey this book takes its readers on is a journey into the heart of a treatment process, albeit an imaginary one, where the daily problems that one may encounter on such a programme are worked through using behavioural modification and psychotherapeutic methodology. The book explains what may be going wrong on your programme, what to do to test your assumptions; and what to do when all else has failed. It works from the premise that children with autism are not immune from emotional upsets, and goes on to demonstrate how other forms of interventions can be combined and be shown to have positive results. The case histories within are altered slightly so as not to distort the facts but rather to protect the children from being identified.

Throughout my training in both fields of enquiry I was told repeatedly that these two schools of thought were incompatible. What I found was that those who were saying this were either trained in one area or the other, never both. So I set about combining these two schools of thought, with much success, as can be demonstrated in the accompanying case histories.

INTRODUCTION

The method of treatment within this book is aimed at the non-professional and, as so, is simplistic in its approach.

What I'm about to explain is presented as a guide as you begin this treatment process. It is hoped that by reading this material you will have a clearer understanding of the theories that underpin the therapy, and by so doing, be able to adapt this information according to the child's needs.

The behavioural school of thought is that children on the autistic spectrum have 'poor training', that they have been taught inappropriately, and that this inappropriate behaviour has been accidentally conditioned into them i.e., two things have become associated in the child's mind. And so they set about conditioning new patterns of behaviour into the child's repertoire.

Within the context of my work, what I observed was teams of mostly overworked therapists, due to the lack of trained people in this country, who would come in week after week and run these children through the same routines until the child was blue in the face. The results being that either the child would close down altogether, or their frustration would show through in tantrums. Then in would come the consultant and conclude 'Oh, he's still not getting it, keep at it until he does.' Arrggh!!!

Often the child's abilities were under-pitched, resulting in boredom, and there was seldom an action plan put in place for the team to work to should the child reach their targets beforehand. Treating the symptoms that arose due to this lack of insight and contingency became the main focus.

Brown's tip-of-the-tongue syndrome, in which the child is tempted to finish the word or sentence by giving them the first letter or words, is frequently used. Hence, when you see a sentence with the first letter followed by . . . you'll be able to gauge what is expected of you from the surrounding words.

The psychotherapeutic approach, where the client 'unfolds' at their own pace, is not one that is advocated here, for the child on the spectrum is apt to get stuck and so needs to be nudged into action, enabling them to move forward.

The psychoanalytic model holds with the belief that strong drives within the child are being denied within the social sphere.

The psychoanalytic method of silence and reflection, i.e. the echoing back to the child, is applied whenever possible, with the Kleinian method of quick interpretation being used to address the issues as swiftly as they arise.

The writings of R.D. Laing inspired much of the work, employing Laing's idea of reaching through to an unresponsive client by means of entering into their world, rather than attempting to pull them into ours.

Art and play therapy are the mediums used to help express the child's unconscious conflicts. Interpretation is secondary to expression here, as I believe that no matter how many theories come along and attempt to persuade us that they have the necessary insights into why someone is behaving as they do, all these can really do is to make speculations. No one knows what's really going on within the realms of another, all we can hope is that our assumptions are leading the child in whatever direction is right for them.

The methods explained within this book can, as shown, be used with verbal and non-verbal children.

The therapy within the book is not exhaustive of the various teachings that the child can be exposed to, what is hoped for is that the reader will be better equipped to deal with the various problems that may arise during the teaching. The material contained within gives you a set of tools that can be applied to any other material that you may wish to teach to your child.

What is not promised here is 'a cure' but rather a more adaptive and socially content outcome for the child.

Finally, the author wishes to stress that autism has been shown to be caused by an interplay of many factors, whether your child is at the extreme end of the spectrum or at the milder end can only be discerned through proper diagnosis. Whatever this outcome may be, what can be said of the contents of this book is that your child will have access to this hugely expansive means of intervention, and by so doing they will have a better chance of integrating into their world.

CHAPTER 1

Behavioural intervention explained

One of the most important understandings of behavioural intervention is how to apply differential reinforcement, which means the gradual decreasing of reinforcement. An example of reinforcement is when your child makes a correct response to something you've asked him to do. You then follow this with a reward, which is known as a reinforcer.

Differential reinforcement. Verbal behaviourism

Example

Parent: "Sam, sit down" = request.
Child sits down = compliance.
Parent: "Thank you" = reinforcer.

In differential reinforcement the level of reinforcement is gradually decreased from "Whoopee!"—this being a high level of reinforcement that is aimed at giving the child a good physiological feeling, which corresponds with the correct response—to a slight nod of the head. However, to continue to give such a high level of reinforcement may result in the child becoming over-stimulated or super-saturated (unmotivated to respond at all, as he knows what's coming), and so the reinforcer is then said to have lost its reinforcing value.

So, as a rule, work with lots of enthusiasm and begin to reduce your level of reinforcement as soon as possible. Remember to vary your use of language as much as possible (e.g. super, great, fantastic, terrific, and so on) until eventually a smile or an affirmative nod of the head suffices. This also serves to give the child feedback on his performance.

If a wrong response is given, apply silence. Look away, wait for a couple of seconds and then repeat the instruction.

Practitioners of verbal behaviourism employ something called "errorless teaching". This means that any request given to the child is immediately followed through with the correct response. This is said to help facilitate a correct response from the child, who then knows what's expected of him, and the instructor knows where the child is in terms of knowledge and can test this as follows:

Example

Instructor: "Hey, what's your name?"
Child says nothing. Three seconds elapse.
Instructor: "Say 'Tom'."
Child: "Tom."
Instructor: "Good."
Instructor: "Hey, what's your name?"
Child: "Tom."

The instructor then immediately follows through with the reinforcement, such as saying "Clever child". The child is then distracted for a couple of minutes before being asked the same question again:

Instructor: "What's your name?"
Child: "Tom."

The instructor then delivers huge reinforcement for this independent answer, such as throwing the child in the air while saying, "That's right, your name is Tom."

The reinforcement can be tightened up if need be to give a one second time lapse. However, try not to prolong this timed response for more than five seconds at this stage in the teaching.

The way that the question is asked of the child is an important factor and should vary as much as possible. As you can see from the example used above, the format of the question asked of the child varied immediately, it went from "Hey, what's your name?" to "What's your name?"

At a latter stage the instructor might say: "Are you Tom?" The instructor then immediately follows through with: "Say 'Yes, I'm Tom'." By so doing, he is giving the child the correct usage of language.

The aim of the exercise is to help the child use language correctly. This is done by means of modelling what is expected, and reinforcing it, and in so doing we are giving the child every chance of success and, as a consequence of this, we are also helping to raise his self-esteem. Children are more willing to try when they are receiving positive feedback.

The embedding of the child's name into a sentence as soon as possible helps him to push his expectations of himself and this helps to keep the programme from stagnation, and the child from closing down through boredom.

This stretching of the teaching unit helps pitch the teaching at a realistic level, which can be reduced if necessary, and does not underestimate the child's ability.

If the child is given the correct usage of language from the start, then his chances of imitating this (rather than sound bites of language, which appear artificial and robotic) are greatly improved.

So instead of responding with "Tom", the instructor says: "Yes, you're TOM," embedding the target word "TOM" within the language structure straight away, while using voice inflection to emphasise the target word (in this case, "Tom").

Remember, the key to a successful programme is to tailor it to suit the individual needs of the child.

CHAPTER 2

Constructing the learning environment

Apparatus

A small table and two chairs. The chairs should be small enough for the child to get up into and sturdy enough for the instructor to sit in.

Stimulus

Toys; small ones are usually easier for the tutors to manipulate, such as bubbles, balloons, and small pieces of fruit or chocolate, (about 1cm in size). Notice that we mentioned the healthier option first, but if your child likes chocolate, then go for it.

Please don't beat yourself up about giving your child their favourite snack, as this is the key to any reinforcement, whatever works as a reinforcer on any particular day use it!

Reinforcement

Reinforcement should be given within one to five seconds after a response.

If the skill is one that we know the child knows, then we can give the child what is referred to as 'processing time', anything up to 10 seconds. However, when the skill is still on acquisition then the rule of one to five seconds applies.

Reinforcers, as the name suggests, should be just that: REINFORCING! To give an example, if on every occasion I saw you, you waved to me, then the chances are that I would wave back at you. However, if I did not respond to your waving by waving back, then more than likely you would cease waving to me.

If I had responded to your waving, then I would have been reinforcing your behaviour. Then it could be said that your behaviour had influenced my behaviour, which in turn influenced your behaviour.

If, however, I ignored your waving, and you then stop waving at me, then my behaviour would have influenced your behaviour, i.e. you stopped waving.

Extinction burst

The example given is of a worst-case scenario where the child is refusing to attend.

This is often the first thing to encounter in any teaching and, if dealt with correctly, should not present as a problem—if it does, this is a signal that something is wrong on the programme.

What to expect from an extinction burst:

Example

Your child is politely and firmly asked:

Instructor: "Come here."

The child responds by immediately dropping to his knees, throwing himself on the floor and thrashing around, screaming and crying.

As yet nobody has done anything, except to request the child to "Come here".

The child's response is an example of an extinction burst in full throttle.

Ordinarily the adults present give in to the child or enter into a discussion with the child. This is not the way forward, as it allows for task avoidance and reinforces the negative behaviour.

The next time the child decides to refuse your request he will exhibit even more extremes of behaviour. Always try to follow through with whatever you've asked the child to do; if not immediately, then certainly before they are allowed to leave the teaching environment. Remember to give high reinforcement only for uncorrected responses.

So in dealing with any negative behaviour, start as you mean to go on: praise the best and ignore the rest. Set the ground rules at the start and you will save yourself a lot of time and effort.

How to deal with an extinction burst

Begin by asking the child: "Come here." If he refuses at this stage, test to see why. For example, if when you walk out of the room the child follows, you can be sure that he is looking for a reaction from you. If, however, they stay where they are, then the behaviour is aimed at task avoidance.

In this case, the instructor should lift the child into the chair (screaming and all) and act as though he were doing nothing wrong. He may kick, bite, or scratch, and probably will. Remember not to look at the child or speak to him while an extinction burst is in full swing; in fact, apply this rule whenever your child refuses a request.

All instructions should be followed through, even if this means carrying the child to the chair and holding him in the sitting position until he is sitting in the chair, this you do for a count of five, then reinforce this, and then let him go. This should proceed something like this:

Instructor: "Good sitting," and holds the child in the chair for a count of five. Then you let the child go from the chair, which is reinforcing in itself. Let the child wander around for a while as they try to figure out what just happened.

A few minutes later, repeat the drama again, only this time hold the child in the sitting position for a count of 10. Repeat this process over and over, with short breaks in between. Try using different people, each slightly prolonging the time spent in the chair. When the child is released, they are then interacted with as normal, with no mention as to what just happened.

Remember to give the child no additional language, nor eye contact, until he is coming and sitting without protest. Within two or three days, and certainly no more than two weeks, your child should be presenting at the table perfectly.

When the extinction burst has been dealt with and the child is coming to the chair on the first request, then the instructor can reinforce the child with a small toy, or blow bubbles, maybe even pull a funny face—whatever entertains the child, but for only short bursts of time.

The instructor should keep control of the reinforcer at all times, and the child should only be allowed access to each reinforcer for short periods, which enables the reinforcer to remain reinforcing.

Special items of interest can be set aside for use on the programme, but these should not be made available to the child outside of therapy time.

The people involved in the programme are also 'reinforcer' and the child should seek them out for fun activities. Try to think of all the time spent with the child as teaching time. The guidelines for structured teaching should, whenever possible, be applied also in the natural environment.

What to do if the child gets up from the table

In this situation the instructor asks the child: "Come here." If he refuses the request, bring him back to the table without saying anything, or looking at him, and remember not to show any reaction.

Repeat the original instruction and "hand over hand" (referred to in the rest of the book as HOH) guide the child back to the table, then slightly reinforce this and allow him to leave the table.

Occupy the child for a few minutes with a task such as a jigsaw puzzle, which should be "backward chained", in that the puzzle should have been completed beforehand, with one piece remaining to be done.

Then the instructor says: "Let's do the puzzle." The child then picks up the remaining piece of puzzle and places it in the appropriate hole. This is then reinforced, the instructor making a huge fuss of the child.

Always let the child go on a positive note so that his last recollection of the teaching time is positive. If the child has not managed to give a correct response then help him to do so; HOH guide him to do this if necessary, and then reinforce this before letting him go from the task. We then guide the child back to the less preferred task, i.e. the one they tried to avoid at the table.

As you end your teaching, so you begin it. By this I mean that you start on a known response and end on a known response, and by so doing you are positively reinforcing the child as he begins and as he ends. The child should feel as though he is having a ball and be eager to engage in his programme.

Remember that the child must follow through on all instructions, so if the instructor says "Go and play", then the child must go and play. If he resists this, give him a gentle nudge to do so, for whenever the child is in teaching time the child 'must' comply with what the instructor says, even if HOH is necessary to help him to do so; or else the child ends up taking control of the situation and a battle of wills begins.

Gradually the child will have the amount of demands placed upon him increased. Let the child be your guide in this—if he will happily sit for three requests, then let this be your maximum.

Also, let the programme be flexible in any teaching unit:

Example

1. Come to the table.
2. Put two pieces of jigsaw together.
3. Touch the child's nose.

The instructions given should go something like this:

Instructor: "Come here."
Child complies.
Instructor: "Hey, nice, come here."
Instructor: "Do the puzzle."
Child complies.
Instructor: "Well done."
Instructor: "Can you touch your nose?"
Child ignores the instruction.
The instructor HOH guides the child to touch their nose and continues:
Instructor: "Good, touching your nose."
Instructor: "Touch your nose."
Child complies.
Instructor: "Good, can you touch the puzzle?"
Child complies.
Instructor: "Well done, can you touch you nose?"
Child complies.
Instructor: "Hurray, you can go and play."
Child goes and plays for a few minutes.

Instructor: "Come here."
Child complies.
Instructor: "Thank you for coming, can you touch your nose?"
Child complies.
Instructor: "Excellent," and gives the child a small piece of chocolate.
Instructor: "Can you clap?"
Child complies.
Instructor: "Touch your nose."
Child complies.
Instructor: "Hey! That was terrific, go and play."

In this example the child is already on a roll, having given a correct response independently. This was then highly reinforced. The instructor then stretched the reinforcement to encompass two responses ("Can you clap?" and "Touch your nose").

Notice that no reinforcement was given after the request "Can you clap?". The child was then asked for a second response, "Touch your nose". Only then was he given the reinforcement.

The child should "know" the responses that he is being asked for, i.e. the clap, touching his nose. This is an example of differential reinforcement being applied.

Eventually more and more responses will be required of the child before the reinforcement is given, so that rather than reinforcing every response the child can give a chain of responses before receiving his reinforcer. Eventually the child will be weaned off reinforcement altogether.

Language should be kept fairly simple at this stage so as not to hinder the child's processing of the information and instructions should not be repeated over and over.

If the child is non-compliant, look away and wait for about five seconds, before repeating the instruction. Often the tendency is to keep repeating the command because it seems as though the child didn't hear, or has forgotten what was said to him, but it may well be task avoidance, so a non-response should be treated as an incorrect response.

Some behaviourists advocate using what is called the discrete trial approach, in which the child is given feedback on his performance.

Example

Instructor: "Come here."
Child does nothing.
Instructor: "No."
Instructor: "Come here."

Here, the non-response is treated as an incorrect response. The "No" is said to be giving the child feedback concerning whether he did, or did not, get it right. However, if you cast your memory back to the example earlier about you waving to me, and me ignoring you, no one had to say "No" for you to understand that I was not giving you the required response. Your behaviour reflected this.

To hear "No" too often may result in the child's self-esteem being lowered, and if heard often enough the child may well shut down altogether. So let your silence be his guide and if the item is known to the child then let him have processing time of about 10 seconds. Be flexible with this, as in all things, so that the child doesn't get set in patterns of responding behaviour.

The child's reasoning goes something like: "I can now estimate how long I can hold out on my responding time, so I'll just amuse myself."

Extinction bursts will tell us if everything is going well.

CHAPTER 3
Teaching a three-year-old

This chapter is aimed at teaching a child of three years old. These small movements are the building blocks for the more complex skills that our child will be required to make at a later date. These are the skills that will enable him to function independently in his world.

Techniques

Begin with a simple instruction:

Instructor: "Do this," and places a small block into a bowl.

The child is then HOH guided to perform this action, while the instructor simultaneously repeats the instruction. On its completion we continue:

Instructor: "Well done," and blows bubbles.
Instructor: "Do this," and models the behaviour for the child to imitate. This time no HOH is given.
The child attempts to lift the block and put it in the bowl.
Instructor: "Nice try."
Instructor: "Do this," and models the behaviour again.
This time the child succeeds in completing the action unaided.
Instructor: "Fantastic!" and blows some more bubbles.

There are many variations of movements, and all should be practiced singularly to begin with, each one being reinforced to ensure mastery. Then the instructor should stretch the reinforcement to include two or more commands. Keep including other movements into the chain, until the child can complete all of these before he is given any reinforcement. Vary these as much as possible, so the child remains challenged and does not become bored.

When a particular movement is clear and precise, then you add another to your chain, which you continue mixing and matching.

Example

The instructor sits on the left-hand side of a right-handed child and to the right of a left-handed child. The instructor then models the correct behaviour for the child to follow.

Instructor: "Do this," and places their right palm on the table, while HOH guiding the child to do the same, i.e. using your right hand, put the child's right hand on the table top while holding their left hand with your left hand.
Instructor: "Yes!"

Repeat the task and if the child tries but is unable to complete the action precisely, say words to the effect of: "That was a good try."
Repeat as before and when the child gives the correct response say "Excellent!" and give him a small piece of fruit.

Example of a reinforcement schedule

Instructor: "Yes," and does not give the child a piece of fruit.

Then the instructor says nothing and gives the child a piece of fruit. (Remember to give only small pieces of whatever you are reinforcing the child with, so they stay motivated by it.)
To decide on which reinforcer the child wants, hold up two items at a time, and put the one they reach for to one side. Then hold another item up with the less preferred one and so on, until you have a hierarchy of reinforcers. If the child doesn't reach for an item, put it to one side and keep going until you find something he is interested in. This is not always easy, however, but by watching your child you will eventually come to see what he is interested in. This might not seem interesting to you, but remember, it's the child's choice, so go with it.
Even if this is twiddling his fingers in front of his face, turn this to your advantage and use it as your reinforcer. Say to the child "You can do this, but first we are going to do this." Then, when he does as you asked, let him twiddle his fingers in front of his face, allowing him access to this behaviour as you would any other reinforcer. Then block this and redirect the child with something that is incompatible with the finger-twiddling.

The next teaching trial

Instructor: "Do this," and models lifting their hand up from the table as if making a stop sign, i.e. palms facing outwards.
Child copies.
Instructor: "You've got it," and tickles the child.

Then continue with an array of movements, such as:

Both hands on the table facing downward;
One hand up and one hand down;
Tapping the table with one hand then two;
Hands together as in prayer;
A single clap.
Clapping first at a normal pace, then slowly, then fast, and with arms stretched out to the sides to produce an exaggerated form of clapping.
Remember to vary the way that you ask them to do a thing.

Example

Do this. copy me, try this, can you do this? How about that?

The thumbs-up sign is something that people often have difficulty teaching, so we shall proceed by showing you how to shape this using forward chaining.

1.   Begin with both hands face down on the table. Reinforce.
2.   Hold both hands up, as in the stop sign. Reinforce.
3.   Spread the fingers wide apart. Reinforce.
4.   Close the fingers together again. Reinforce.
5.   Move the hands together until the tips of the thumbs touch. Reinforce.
6.   Make a fist with the fingers.
7.   Move one hand away. Lo and behold we are left with the thumbs-up sign.

Begin by reinforcing the child at every stage, as well as when he's making an effort to do the movement. HOH him if necessary, then hold the movement while simultaneously reinforcing him. Then chain these together. The chaining should proceed something like this:

Example

Instructor: "Do this."

1. Hands face down on the table. Reinforce.

Instructor: "Do this."

2. Hands down on the table, lift the hands up. Reinforce.

Instructor: "Do this."

3. Hands face down on the table, lift the hands up, and spread the fingers wide apart. Reinforce.

Instructor: "Do this."

4. Hands face down on the table, lift the hands up, spread the fingers wide apart, and close the fingers. Reinforce.

Instructor: "Do this."

5. Hands down on the table, lift the hands up, spread the fingers wide apart, close the fingers, move the hands together until the thumbs touch. Reinforce.

Instructor: "Do this."

6. Hands down on the table, lift the hands up, spread the fingers wide apart, close the fingers, move the hands together until the thumbs touch, move the touch thumbs together until they touch, make a fist with the fingers. Reinforce.

Instructor: "Do this."

7. Hands face down on the table, lift hands up, spread fingers wide apart, close fingers, move the thumbs together until they touch, make a fist with the fingers, separate the hands, move one hand away. Hey presto, you have a thumbs-up.

This procedure can also be used for the pointing response, beginning with the index fingers on the sides of a table, as though playing the piano with one finger, the other fingers are then tucked under and out of the way, then lift the index fingers like candles and then position them at an angle of 45 degrees and reinforce this until we have the pointing sign. From then on we can instruct the child: "Point to the . . ."

Try to make pointing fun, such as pretending to be shooting objects with your finger. Hold up finger puppets, and as the child pretends to shoots at them with a pointed finger, put the puppets down one at a time.

Singing songs where the child has to perform actions is a fun way for them to practice their gross and fine motor skills. You and your child will have your own favourites.

The children's game of pat-a-cake is best not incorporated into these actions for the time being, because it tends to hinder the process—what may happen is that when you eventually position yourself in front of the child to have him imitate you from this angle, instead of holding his hands up in stop signs in imitation of you, he tries to play pat-a-cake. It's worth watching out for this.

Build your sequences one by one, as in the thumbs, then on to the index fingers, followed by different variations of fingers. When the child has completed these single actions, begin then to chain them together, first two at a time as in:

Instructor: "Do this" and claps, then puts their index fingers together.
Child claps.
Instructor: "Ok."
The child then follows through with the second action, putting their index fingers together.
Instructor: "You did it!"

A two-part reinforcement

Continue on, and lengthen the reinforcement as follows:

Instructor: "Do this" and models the clap and touching all finger-tips together.
The child then completes both of the instructions one after the other.

17

Instructor: "Hurray!" and throws the child into the air as a reward for this chained response.

The child then gets released from the teaching situation and has 10 minutes of guided play. This can be anything the child likes doing, from jumping on a small trampoline or playing peak-a-boo—anything that seems age-appropriate and which *is* appropriate.

YOU be the judge of what is appropriate. Rocking the child to and fro would be inappropriate. Guide him to a swing, or a Swiss exercise ball. Here the child is strengthening his wrists and spine and still having fun. Having wheelbarrow races serves the same purpose.

Please remember that the child must be attending well before any demands are placed upon him. Simply say something to the effect of "Sit nicely, please," and reinforce this behaviour, before asking the child to comply with any other activity.

This reinforcing of good sitting can be applied when the child is not complying with a given request. In this instance, the non-compliant behaviour is being ignored while you concentrate on reinforcing the good behaviour, the sitting.

As most behaviour is attention-seeking or avoidance, the child will eventually cotton on to the fact that he gets attention for good behaviour and so comply, similarly when he tries to avoid a situation, he nevertheless is still required to do it. So the child's logic is, best do it, and then I can get my own way.

Try to think of the natural world also as the teaching environment, so whenever you catch the child sitting nicely etc, give him the thumbs-up sign and say: "That's nice sitting." Now he feels good about himself and can see how the thumbs-up action is used in the real world.

Remember to keep your language simple and begin to point things out to them in the natural world, such as "Look, I see a giraffe," when visiting the zoo. "What can you see? Point and show me."

So now you have been introduced to differential reinforcement, and are familiar with the building up of items in order to chain these together, and our child now has a small repertoire of movements.

Apply the same procedures for the arms and legs. Begin by having your child standing by your side, to the left or right depending on which hand they use. When raising your right arm, they must raise their right arm, and the same goes for the legs.

Standing in front of the child is a bit trickier as he is now copying your opposite sides, a bit confusing but he will get it. Just don't underestimate his intelligence.

To make sure the child is getting precise actions, have him hold the movement for a count of three, this can then be prolonged before reinforcing him.

If you find that the child is having difficulty holding his arms up straight then place an exercise band or tie a scarf around his arms. If the difficulty is in holding his arms out to the sides, you can assist this by placing the child against a wall or have him sit in a winged chair and gently press the arms back. Here the action is aided by the props, which help to prevent the arms from going too far back or forwards.

If the problem is with the legs, and the child is having difficulty standing on one leg, then help him by putting a small stool slightly behind him, then place one of his feet flat on the stool, while he balances on the other foot. If need be, stand in front of him and hold his hands to help with balance. Reinforce this to a count of five, that you then prolong and in time move the stool away. This movement is the prerequisite for the hop.

To help the child going up and down the stairs on alternate feet, block them from putting both feet on the same step at the same time by holding the stationary foot with your foot then reinforce this, and when their other foot reaches the next step, as initially guided by you, reinforce again.

To help a child put on a coat, the Montessori system, where the coat is placed on the floor in front of the child with the armholes at the bottom, is by far the easiest way. The child just puts his arms into the armholes and, in one movement, throws the coat over his head, pulling his arms through as he does so. Model this for him.

The spooning of broad beans from one bowl into another, or emptying lentils from one plastic jug into another, is good for hand-eye co-ordination and helps with the feeding process. Make sure that the ingredients you use are not something the child is allergic to, and please stay with them whenever they are doing these things in case of choking.

How to ride a tricycle

To accustom your child to their new toy, first have them stand beside the object and begin to talk to them about it: "Look at your nice silver tricycle." Press the bell, let them press it etc, all the while giving him small pieces of fruit or whatever, so that an item they enjoy (the fruit) becomes associated with the new, unfamiliar object (the tricycle).

If the child is too scared to sit on the tricycle at first, begin by showing him another child having fun on a tricycle, you can then pretend to sit on the tricycle or have his favourite teddy bear sitting on it.

Make it seem like huge fun to ride a tricycle: "Vroom vroom, beep beep, here comes teddy," and so on.

When the time comes and the child approaches the tricycle on his own, reinforce this, as any movement towards the object is a step in the right direction. Have a jellybean on the seat of the tricycle as this will act as an incentive for the child to get closer.

Remember to reinforce any movement towards the object and, if you can, have two tricycles available, then when your child is all excited about going to the park present the little companion who is all ready outside on their tricycle with your child's new tricycle standing nearby.

Say something such as: "Come on, let's go, quickly, get on your tricycle." Then lift the child onto the tricycle, ignoring any protest, just keep going, and then—after the protest has stopped, usually they are too concerned with staying on—as quickly as you lifted them on, lift them off again. Make no mention to what just happened.

Repeat this activity while at the park. Quickly lift the child onto the tricycle and say:

Instructor: "And away we go, whoopee!" Reinforce every single press down on the pedal. Then prolong the reinforcement and keep reassuring the child in a calm voice, saying how brave he is and how good he is at riding the tricycle. Placing books under the stabilisers will help the child make the pedalling motion while remaining stationary.

In situations where the child is a bit scared, keep the reinforcement low-key, intermittently reassuring them as such in a gentle, calming voice.

When they seem to be ready to dismount, take them off before they have a chance to ask to be taken off—pre-empting any resistance is far better than having to deal with protest. Please do not insist that they remain on the tricycle for "Just a little bit longer" as this can be counter-productive

Socialisation

To help the child learn to wait, put something he wants in front of him on the table. Make sure the child can't reach the item.

Example

Instructor: "Wait," and waits for five seconds.
The child reaches for the activity, the instructor blocks this with their arm.
Instructor: "Let's try that again."
Instructor: "Wait," and repeats the procedure.
Child complies.
Instructor: "Good waiting!" and lets the child have access to the item.

Passing a beanbag around a circle of people also helps the child to learn to wait for longer intervals. Have the beanbag stop at them as reinforcement.

Standing in line and waiting is a progression of the wait programme. This is a very important skill for the child, as he needs to respond, and respond quickly to the command "WAIT!" The child must be prevented from running onto a busy road, for instance.

Begin your teaching with the child by your side and say:

Instructor: "Wait!"
As the child begins to move forward, stop him from doing so. Then let the child walk a little farther and again give the instruction:

Instructor: "Wait."
Child continues on.
The instructor then brings the child back to the point where they were at when the instruction was initially given, and repeats the command "Wait!" while preventing the child from moving forward. Hold this for a few seconds then reinforce this waiting before letting the child continue.

Repeat this programme as often as necessary and prolong the length of time that the child has to wait. Vary this from time to time. Do this programme using all the adults whom the child has access to and begin to extend the distance that the child travels before shouting, "Wait". If the child enters mainstream school, the wait command can then be shouted across a busy playground.

Keep extending the distance and begin to say '"Wait" in a lower tone of voice. The wait programme can also be transferred to the child's scooter and tricycle.

When wishing to bring the child towards you, wait until you are close before asking him to come to you, then you are in a position to prevent him running off, or else he is liable to take off like a shot.

Directions

Example

Instructor: "Do this," claps and goes to the door and knocks.
Instructor: "Do this," claps and then takes the child to the door and (HOH) they knock at the door.
Instructor: "You try," and imitates clapping.
Child claps and the instructor leads him to the door and, together (HOH) they knock at the door.
Instructor: "That was amazing!"
Instructor: "Do this," and claps and goes to knock on the door.
Child completes the two commands.
Instructor "You were amazing," and gives the child a sweet.

The child can then be released from the teaching trial. Shorten the distance that the child has to go if necessary, as sometimes the child does the first action and then wanders off en route to the second. If this happens, bring the child back to the beginning and repeat the instruction as in the initial trial. The sequence can, if necessary, be broken down into two stages, with reinforcement following on from each, until the child can complete both consecutively.

If the child does the second instruction, forgetting the first, then break the sequence down by asking for the clap, and then reinforce this, before asking for the second. If the child is verbal, ask them to repeat the instruction back to you, and as they do so hold up one finger for the first thing, then another finger for the second thing. Then as the child completes each instruction lower your fingers one at a time. This acts as a guide for the child who looks to the fingers as a source of remembering, regarding how many things he was asked to do. Reinforcement should be high for any unaided successes.

This programme eventually has more sequences added to it, for instance: "Turn around and put the book on the table." "Stand on one leg, then go to the TV and come back." These combined actions are then chained together, so the child must listen and follow as directed.

Receptive language

To begin, get yourselves two similar decks of picture cards, the bigger the better, so the child can see the contents. As time goes on use smaller cards, as this forces the child to look closer at what is being presented to them and helps them take in more detail.

Start by calling the child to the table. Here is their first correct response, so reinforce this. When the child is seated at the table, have one of the cards face up in front of him and give him a similar card.

Instructor: "Match," and (HOH) guides the child to place their card on top of the card on the table.
Instructor: "Terrific!"

The next stage is to put two different cards on the table, and give one similar card to the child.

Instructor: "Match."
The child now has a choice of two cards. Here the real learning begins.

The child should be blocked from placing his card on the wrong card and highly reinforced for the correct response. Then switch the cards around, so that the child is not just going to the same place and guessing. Try holding the cards up in front of the child and ask him to touch the correct card.

Present the cards again at the table, and move the pictures around. If the child does not respond (HOH) guide their hand to touch the requested item and reinforce.

Now for some of that differential reinforcement that we spoke of earlier. Instead of guiding their hand (HOH), point to the correct item, or nod your head in that direction. Alternatively you can nudge their arm in the right direction, or look at the item being asked for. Be careful with this one, as even experienced instructors can inadvertently prompt a given response by quickly glancing in the direction of the item they are asking for.

Do not give a big reinforcer for any response, which has to be assisted, only give edibles or toys for unaided responses. So if the child gets it almost right, praise them (e.g. "Nice try") or you can bring the reinforcer nearer to them.

The matching should then include un-identical items, such as two pictures of different cats. This procedure can be used for colour, number, shape, and people.

The knowing of body parts is often tricky for children on the spectrum, whose sense of proprioception (where their body is in space) is often muddled.

Some of the children have difficulty saying and doing at the same time, so to help them with this, we can ask them to drum on a drum, or on the floor, while saying silly things such as "Boom boom tacka tacka boom boom up!"

Instructor: "Copy me," and models the behaviour and language for the child to copy.
This, and similar, are ways around this particular deficit.

To enable the child to know and label parts of his body, the instructor can start by using himself as the object to be touched, as demonstrated here:

Instructor: "Where is my nose?" and (HOH) guides the child to touch his nose. Reinforce this.
Instructor: "Where is your nose?" and then guides the child through the action and reinforces.

All the body parts should be worked through until these can be chained together, as in: "Can you touch your/my nose, eyes, mouth?" This is also helping the child with their personal pronouns (my/yours).

A large drawing of a child, or a teddy bear, can be of aid when teaching body parts.

Example

Instructor: "Where is the teddy's head?"
The child is then guided through the motion.

We can then chain these actions together and present them as fast as possible. The nursery rhyme "Head, shoulders, knees and toes" is useful for this.

Comparisons

A child of three is able to compare objects and to help our child to do this we present him with an array of objects and (HOH) guide him to pick up the correct ones.

Instructor: "Touch the one that is round."

When the child has been taught these items, move them on to the next stage:

Instructor: "Point to the one that looks like a wheel."

The instructor should present this programme in as many different ways as he can think of, using shape, colour, food, clothes, vehicles, and so on, finally ending up with:

Instructor: "Point to the one that is NOT round" etc.
Here the instructor is giving the correct language to the child.
Instructor: "This one is NOT round."
Instructor: "Touch the one that isn't round."
Child touches the one that isn't round.
Instructor: "Yes, that one isn't round. Well done."

Stephanie Louise

The child will eventually group objects into categories and to do this the instructor sits with the child on the floor (to vary the place where the stimulus is presented) and in front of them has three items or three 2D cards. Do not use too many to begin with, three to five in a category is enough. The child then has three corresponding pictures in front of him; one contains clothes, the other vehicles, and a third foodstuffs. The instructor then gives the child one item that corresponds to one of the piles.

Instructor: "Sort," and guides the child to the correct picture and yet again reinforces the correct action. If the child gets it wrong the instructor then (HOH) guides him through the procedure and again reinforces this, before asking for the same item again.

To expand this programme we give the child a small pile of items, and say: "Sort these." Alternately we can have an array of items, say three from each of the chosen categories, and we can say to the child:

Instructor: "Give me all the animals/clothes/foods."

This programme leads nicely to the "Not" programme. Here the child is given two categories and asked which ones are NOT for eating. This is then expanded to include driving, using vehicles, wearing, using clothes, and so on.

The understanding of the opposite terms such as empty/full, heavy/ light, wet/dry, and same/different can be taught as follows.

Example

The instructor gives the child a small piece of velvet and a piece of sandpaper, and requests:

Instructor: "Point to the soft one" or "Touch the rough one."

The instructor then points to the velvet or sandpaper and the child is directed to touch or point to the correct item.

Similarly, the word "heavy" can be taught using a small container of sand and an empty container, while for wet/dry use two pieces of paper towel, one wet, the other dry.

Same/different

The same / different programme is presented in this format: three apples and one orange are placed in front of the child and the instructor says:

Instructor: "Which are the same?" "Which one is different?" "Which one is the odd one out?" "Give me the one that's different." "Touch the different one." "Pick out the one that 's not the same." "Can you show me the one that's the odd one out?"

To help the child along it's best to start with items that are very different. This can then transform into something similar to the "Sort" programme, using piles of toy vehicles, cars, helicopters or hairbrushes, and toothbrushes etc, always remembering that variety is the spice of life.

Inferences

For inferences, the tutor can use real life or cards. Things in the real world, as opposed to 2D stimuli, are helpful in that they make the programme seem more real for the child and as such should be promoted as much as possible.

Example

Instructor: "Is daddy home?" and points to daddy's car in the driveway, saying: "Yes, daddy is home, there is his car."

Alternatively we can show the child pictures of a person dripping wet in a swimsuit, and a boy wrapped up for winter, and then continue:

Instructor: "Which boy has been swimming?" and points to the card with the boy who is dripping wet. "This is the boy who has been swimming, look he's all wet."
Instructor: "Where is the boy who has been swimming?" and guides the child to the picture of the boy who is wet.
Instructor: "Yes, that's the boy who has been swimming."
Instructor: "Pick the boy who's been swimming."

Child does nothing.
Instructor: "Pick the boy who has been swimming," and (HOH) touches the correct card. "You've got it."
Instructor: "Find the boy who has been swimming," and looks at the correct picture.
Child follows the instructor's gaze and touches the correct picture.
Instructor: "Brilliant."

The instructor now switches the positions of the cards, and again asks the child to find the picture of the boy who has been swimming. If the child gets it right, reinforce him with a tangible reinforcer, such as something to play with or eat.

If the child does not get it right, then repeat the procedure, mixing it between things that the child already knows.

Example

Instructor: "Find the boy who has been swimming."
Child does nothing.
Instructor: "Wave, touch your head."
Child complies.
Instructor: "Well done."
Instructor: "Point to the boy who has been swimming."

If the child is verbal, ask him to say yes or no to the question:

Instructor: "Has the boy been swimming?"
The instructor then says: "Yes, the boy has been swimming, that's why he's all wet."
Instructor: "How do we know the boy has been swimming? Because he's all w . . ."
Child: "Wet."
Instructor: "Correct! Well done!"

Before you start this procedure with a verbal child, ask him to say what he sees in the picture cards before asking questions, as this helps to ensure that he is looking carefully.

Expressive language

A child of three would be able to speak in three-word sentences and so we shall begin to look at some programme ideas to help our child do the same.

Start by acquiring a pack of action cards, or pictures from a catalogue where people are doing things, or you can draw these, then we can present our child with some action pictures.

Example

The instructor shows the child a picture of someone riding a bike and asks:

Instructor: "What's the girl doing?" and "Girl riding bike."
Child attempts to repeat.
Instructor: "Nice try."
Instructor: "Say 'Girl'."
Child: "Girl."
Instructor: "Yes!"
Instructor: "Say 'Riding'."
Child: "Riding."
Instructor: "Great!"
Instructor: "Say 'Bike'."
Child: "Bike."
Instructor: "That's very good."
Instructor: "Say 'Girl riding'."
Child: "Girl riding."
Instructor: "You're doing so well!"
Instructor: "Say 'Girl riding bike'."
Child: "Riding bike."
Instructor: "Almost there."
Instructor: "Girl."
Child: "Girl."
Instructor: "Riding bike."
Child: "Riding bike."
Instructor: "Magic."
Instructor: "Say 'Girl riding bike'."

Child: "Girl riding bike."
Instructor: "You were supercalifragilisticexpialidocious" and bounces the child on their knee.

As you can see, patience is the order of the day.

If your child is a late talker, we must begin to persuade them to use their words. Often a child with autism pulls people towards the thing he wants and gestures towards it. This must be dissuaded. Ask the child to point to the object they want then:

Instructor: "Say my name."
Child says the instructor's name.
Instructor: "Yes Tom, what do you want?"
Instructor: "Say 'Come with me'."
Child: "Come with me."
Instructor: "Fantastic talking, come and show me what you want."

Ask the child to use their words in many different ways; play with me, chase me, and so on. If your child is not talking at all, begin by having him sitting on your lap with a large mirror facing you both, then make exaggerated mouth movements for him to copy.

The aim of this exercise is for the child to exercise his tongue and lips. Here are some exercises for you to practice:

La La La La La La La La La La La La.
La La La La La La La La
La La La La La La La La

Then repeat these, changing the beginning letter to N, T, and then D.

Examples

Na Na , Ta Ta , Da Da.

The following sounds should be make in varying patterns and said softly, and are shown in capital letters because they are characteristically more weighty and longer in length:

Ah, as in father; Ay, as in pay; Ee, as in ease.

Reinforce each as soon as the child makes the correct sound. If he does not make the sound correctly or makes no sound at all, then look away for three seconds and repeat. If the child still does not make the correct sound move on to the next one.

If the child is refusing to comply with the instruction, do some fast-paced fillers to distract them, along the lines of:

Instructor: "Do this and this and this" while he touches his head, claps, and taps his chest. He then asks for the target again. All in quick succession, remember.

Example

Instructor: "Do this," and touches his head, "and this," and pulls his ear lobes, "and say 'Ee'."

This is usually all it takes to bring the child back on task and can be mixed and matched with any targets that the child is familiar with.

The shorter vowels such as a (as in hat), e (as in pen), and I (as in pin) have a lighter feel to them. Other vowels are OO (as in boot), oo (as in book), OH (as in boat), Aw (as in ball), o (as in box), AH (as in bath), u (as in but), ER (as in bird), AY (as in bake), and EE (as in bead).

To clarify, the long vowels are; OO, OH, AW, AH, ER, AY, and EE. The short vowels are; oo, o, u, a, e, and i. Compound vowels are where movement is required, such as: i (as in high), ow (as in how), oi (as in hoist), and u (as in hue), OOR (as in poor), ORE (as in door), AIR (as in hair), EAR (as in hear), OUR (as in flower), IRE (as in hire), and URE (as in sure).

More exercises

HAH HOO, HAH HOO, HAH-OO, HOW.
Huh hi, Huh hi, huh-i, High.
HAW hi, HAW Hi, HAW-i, Hoist.

Hi HOO, hi HOO, Hi-OO, Hue.
I, as in tin.

Continue with words that contrast, such as; player, flare, really, rarely, dyer, dire, mower, more, higher, hire, vial, vile, layer, and lair. To ensure that the child is making the correct mouth movements you may like to try using a bone prop.

The consonants that a child of three is expected to be able to produce consistently are; m, n, ng, p, f, h, and w. These, then, are your first targets, they can be voiced or unvoiced or a combination of both.

With the voice training being an ongoing process, it is advisable to move forward as soon as the child is able, alternatively you may need to hold back on some of these until the child is ready. This is what is referred to as 'tailoring your programme to suit your child'. There is no magic, the only requirement being common sense.

Stay with your targets as long as you see fit, and move them on when you see that the child is able to do so. Try not to stay with the same target for too long, as the child is apt to close down on you. Try catching him unawares, such as when he is on a roll with some other task and is just about to finish, tag on "Oh, and can you say . . . ?"

Knowing the capabilities of ordinary children is your yard-stick, but this is not something that is set in stone, because children, all being unique, are ready at different times for their developmental milestones to be met. Children don't just wake up one morning and suddenly everything fits into place. If only!

Many a child on the autistic spectrum has outstanding skills in areas where other children in their age bracket lag behind but, unfortunately, language is not usually one of them. If your child is one of those who is ahead in their language then great, just be ready to move them on using the next level, which includes the letters, y, k, b, d, g, and r. These are aimed at the four-year-old, but you can slot them in whenever you see fit.

Lingering too long on skills that the child has quickly mastered can hinder many a programme. If this should happen to you, look at the next level and start there, regardless of the age these are pitched at. Remember, all children are different and all will progress or lag behind in some skill, just be vigilant.

More exercises

Moo Moh Maw, Moo Moh Maw, Moo Moh Maw Moo.
Interchange the beginning letters as in Noo, Poo, Foo, Woo, and Hoo.

Combining tongue and lip movements, progress to:

Loo, Loh, Law, Lah, Lay, Lee.
Again interchange the beginning letters with Noo, Moo, Poo, Boo, Too, Doo, Foo, Voo, and Thoo.

Progress to Oov, Ohv, Awv, Ahv, Ayv, Eev. Similarly with Ook, Oog, Ooth, Oos, Ooz, Oosh (as in shut), Ooge (as in pleasure), Ooch (as in church), Ooj (as in judge), and Ool.

Too Toh Taw Tah Tay Tee
Oot Oht Awt Aht Ayt Eet
Voo Voh Vaw Vah Vay Vee
Oov Ohv Awv Anv Ayv Eev
Zoo Zoh Zaw Zah Zay Zee
Ooz Ohz Awz Ahz Ayz Eez
Choo Choh Chaw Chah Chay Chee
Ooch Ohch Awch Ahch Aych Eech.

Example

Instructor: "Say 'A'."
Child: "Arr."
Instructor looks away for three seconds.
Instructor: "Say 'A'."
Child: "A".
Instructor: "Hey, I knew you could do it," and at the same time gives the child a raisin.

Wait for the child to finish eating and begin the teaching process all over again, eventually chaining these together. The objective is for the child to move through as many as he can, in order to orchestrate the speech instrument to its fullest capacity and by so doing the child gains confidence and clarity.

To prevent the child from getting bored you can ask him for a vowel, then reinforce this, then ask him to imitate an action, then another vowel, and then show him one of the picture cards. Mixing and matching helps break the monotony.

Vary the presentation but try to keep the teaching simple to begin with, as the child may close down for fear of getting it wrong. If this should happen, go back to the beginning and ask for one thing at a time, then begin to build up your sequence once again.

When your child has mastered these, prolong the reinforcement from one second to three, and so on. Then add two in the sequence, then three, then more, until all in the list of items have been mastered. This can be a slow process but one that's very worthwhile—just stay with an item until it's mastered.

Children of three begin to tell of remote events and so must our little one, so try this exercise.

The instructor and child are together in a particular room of the house. The instructor then takes the child into the hallway and brings them back to the original room.

Instructor: "Where did you just go?" followed by "To the hallway."
Instructor: "Where did you just go?"
Child: "To the hall."
Instructor: "Hallway."
Instructor: "Say hall . . ."
Child: "Hallway."
Instructor: "Good."
Instructor: "Where did you just go . . . to the . . . ?"
Child: "Hallway."
Instructor: "Yes, you went to the hallway."
Instructor: "Where did you go . . . to . . ."
Child: "The hallway."
Instructor: "Tremendous!" and gives the child a swing.

Alternatively, when the instructor and child are in the hallway, the instructor can say to the child:

Instructor "Were are we?"
Instructor: "Say 'In the hallway'."
Child: "In the hallway."
Instructor: "Bingo!"

Eventually this programme can be extended to include questions such as: "What did you do there?"

CHAPTER 4
Teaching a four-year-old

The perceptual motor skills for four-year-old children build on those that are already in place for our three-year-old.

Self-help

A four-year-old child is said to be able to wash their own face and hands, as well as dry them.

To begin these self-help skills we shall assume that the wash bowl is too tall for our child to reach, so we need to begin with the placing of a foot-stool at the sink. At this stage we shall go through the entire routine with the child without any reinforcement.

First, the instructor and child stand side by side and the instructor runs through the whole routine:

Instructor: "Wash your hands" and then lifts the footstool and puts it next to the sink, then stands on the stool, then turns on the water, gets the soap, and after this she washes her face and hands, then she puts the soap back and rinses her hands before turning off the tap and then she gets down from the sink and reaches for the hand towel before drying her hands, and finally she puts the towel back in its place.

As you can see there are 12 components to this programme and all must be chained together to achieve the final result.

This goes something like this:

Instructor: "Wash your hands" and (HOH) helps the child to lift the stool and place it next to the sink.
Instructor: "Wonderful" and spins a spinning top on the washroom floor.

On the next occasion when the child is presented with this programme the instructor tests to see what, if anything, the child has retained from the previous trial.

Instructor: "Wash your hands."
Child does nothing.

Instructor: "Wash your hands" and places the child's hands on the footstool before pointing to the place where the footstool goes.
Child lifts the stool and places it near the bottom of the sink.
Instructor: "Pretty good, let's try that again."
Instructor returns the stool to the original position.
Instructor: "Wash your hands" and motions towards the stool.
Child lifts the stool and puts it in the correct place.
Instructor: "Marvellous" and gives the child a piece of chocolate.

The following day the instructor again tests to see how much the child has retained, and all is well. Now the instructor proceeds to the next stage in the programme:

Instructor: "Wash your hands."
Child lifts the stool and places it in the correct position.
Instructor: "Good!" and helps the child step up on the stool. "Fantastic!"

The procedure is repeated, only this time the instructor waits for the child to step up on the stool unaided, before reinforcing. Only if the child does not comply does the instructor help him onto the stool and then slightly reinforces (praises the child but no edible or toy is given).

When presented with the command "Wash your hands", the child is now expected to put two components into the chain: 1. getting the stool and placing it next to the sink; 2. getting onto the stool.

Reinforce this as a two-part reinforcement to begin with, so that as the child completes phase 1 he is praised, then as he completes the second stage unaided he is reinforced a second time.

The next time, when a third component is introduced, the reinforcement is given only after the completion of the first two actions in the chain. Then the child is guided through the third stage, turning on the tap, you then reinforce this, and let the child go from the teaching environment.

At your next teaching trial, the child, when asked "Wash your hands", can now complete stages 1, 2, and 3. The reinforcement should be huge for this independent chain of three actions, such as receiving an ice cream and being allowed to play in the garden.

The next time, when the child is given the command "Wash your hands" he is expected to complete all three stages before the instructor

37

gives any reinforcement. The instructor then guides the child to the fourth stage in the chain. This may only be a pointing to the soap but it may be required that you (HOH) the child. Do not always assume that the child needs the most intrusive guiding, remember that he had the complete sequence shown to him at the beginning of the teaching, and he may well amaze you with what he remembers; sometimes children only need reminding of the ordering of the sequences.

Arts and crafts

To help a child to hold a crayon correctly, try using thick crayons to begin with, as these are far easier for small hands to manipulate. A rubber band secured around the end of a pencil can help to stop their small fingers from slipping. When the child is holding the crayon in the correct position, reinforce this and then gently press their wrist down as they begin to write.

"Copy me" commands are best used to help the child begin to engage in the writing process so, to begin with, the instructor sits on the left side of a right-handed child, each with a piece of A4 paper in front of them, then have the child copy whatever you do.

Start by drawing a straight line from the top of the page down to the bottom.

Example

Instructor: "Do this" and draws a line down the centre of the page.

To aid the child in this process, reach around the back of them with your right arm and (HOH) them to copy what you did. Reinforce the child when they make their best attempt, don't let them become sloppy in their work.

Introduce a horizontal line, a circle, and a cross in the same way.

Pressure is usually a problem for the child so give them lots of hand and wrist strengthening exercises such as; pulling a line of masking tape off a non-carpeted surface, or using large tweezers to pick up beans before putting them into a small bowl, or pulling a pencil through Playdoh. All these are effective ways of strengthening the wrist and pencil grip.

Cutting with scissors is more difficult for the child, as holding the instrument itself can be problematic. Begin by reinforcing the child for just holding the scissors correctly (thumbs down) before asking him to cut anything. When the child is ready to cut, get some light cardboard and draw a thick black line down the middle for him to cut along—this makes the paper easier for them to hold and the line easier for them to follow. In time give them ordinary paper and reduce the thickness of the line. Then introduce zigzag lines, wavy lines, and shapes.

A child of four is able to cut around a circular piece of paper with his thumb upward, and so we can begin to model this action for our child. Let the child draw a circle, then fill it in with clear nail varnish to form a stiff barrier for them to cut and draw around. The varnish applied outside a shape helps him to stay within the boundaries when colouring in. If the nail varnish is not effective, applying glue and glitter will, when hard, serve as a boundary for the child to colour in.

Socialisation

At the age of four a child begins to take an interest in his relatives and associations and joint play then comes into focus and should be encouraged whenever possible.

To encourage playing together with other children, reinforce proximity to begin with. For example, when the two children are playing with different toys but are seated near one another, reinforce this by saying something like: "That's so nice you sitting together." What you are doing is pairing them up. Give them tangible reinforcers and lots of social praise just for being close to each other. The following week try to engage them in joint activities.

Example

Instructor: "Who can guess what I'm drawing?"
Both children guess.
Instructor: "Two winners!" and gives both children a sweet.

To encourage the other child to play with our child, let him win most of the time. Our job now is to teach our child the concept of winning, or else games seem pointless. Keep the interactions quite short to begin with, 15 minutes or so is fine to begin with.

Associations

Buy or draw cards portraying associated items, as these will be required during the table work as we begin to teach our child associations.

Begin with the child seated at the table, and have one card face up on the table in front of him and hold a corresponding card in your hand.

Example

The card on the table has a picture of a fork on it, and the instructor has a card with a picture of a knife on it.

Instructor: "Which one goes with this?" and gives the child their card to put with the one on the table. This is then reinforced and the trial repeated until the child can do this unaided.

This teaching unit is then expanded with two cards on the table. Start with two very different items on the cards to make it easier for the child.

Example

Instructor: "Which ones go together?"

If the child goes for the incorrect card, block him gently with your arm, and guide him to the correct card before reinforcing him. Remember to only give a hug, swing or sweet when the child makes the correct response.

This teaching unit is then expanded to three or more cards. If the cards you are using are extra large, then do the teaching on the floor with the child kneeling in front of them.

Eventually the instructor will use 3D objects to vary the way this teaching unit is presented.

Receptive language

At four years old a child is said to have about 1,500 words in his vocabulary.

We begin to build up our child's vocabulary by teaching them lots of labels, such as garden tools, household appliances, and so on. Try to make these items as functional as possible for the child—if he is not likely to encounter an octopus, and has difficulty saying this, then leave it off your list.

The comparing of animals is something you should include, as these are something the child is apt to need in the natural environment, such as when playing with other children, at the zoo, in his story books and so on.

The next stage for this programme is for the instructor to ask the child: "Touch the one that roars," or, "Which one eats bananas?"

To ensure that our child is listening you can usually get tapes containing animal sounds at your local library. Play the tape to the child, and stop it after each individual animal sound, then ask the child to touch the card that corresponds to the sound that they hear.

Example

The child is seated at the table or in front of the instructor, either the instructor holds up two picture cards with animals on them, or the child can be seated at the table with the two cards in front of him. The tape is then played and an animal sound is heard.

Instructor: "What did you hear?"
Instructor: "A horse, that's what you heard" and (HOH) guides the child to touch the card with the picture of a horse on it. Repeat as necessary and reinforce using differential reinforcement.

An imitation programme, in which the child and instructor take turns being different animals, and each has to guess what the other is, is good for the child as this helps them with body coordination as well as listening skills.

Spatial concepts

Spatial concepts can be taught using small figures that can stand up on their own. The figures are lined up in many different ways, such as in a horizontal line in front of the child, then in a vertical line, or a diagonal. The instructor then begins to ask such questions as: "Who's at the back of the line?" or "Who's at the font of the line?" or "Who's in the middle?"

When the child has mastered this, begin to have them manipulate the figures, for instance "Put the one at the front of the line at the back of the line."

Then our child can be introduced to more complex concepts such as "Put the one with yellow hair at the front of the line," or "Put the small one in front of the one in the middle." 2D cards can also be used to teach this skill.

To introduce this into the natural environment, tell the child such things as: "Today we are going to sit at the back of the bus," or "You sit in the front of the car today."

The concepts of left and right, and night and day, are assumed to be understood by a child of four, and so should be included into your programme. Drawings or cards can be used when asking the child such things as, "When do we go to sleep?", "When do we get up?" and "When do we eat breakfast?"

When starting with left and right, ask the child to show you his left hand or right foot. Alternatively, when the child leaves the house in the morning ask: "Which way are we going, left or right?" Then ask them to point to the right or left, or ask: "Which way is left?" followed by: "And so that way must be? Right".

Example

Instructor: "Which way is right?"
Child points in the correct direction.
Instructor: "Good boy, so that way must be L . . ."
Child: "Left."
Instructor: "Well done!"

Expressive language

Now we are ready to teach our child prepositions; on, behind, next to, in front of.

To do this we start with a chair, on which we place the child's favourite toy. The instructor says to the child, in sequence: "Put teddy on the chair, or beside the chair, next to the chair, in front of the chair." If this seems difficult for the child, have him perform the actions.

Example

Instructor begins with the child standing next to a chair.
Instructor: "Joe, sit on the chair," and sits the child on the chair.
Instructor: "Sit on the chair, good boy."
Instructor: "Sit on the chair," and points to the chair.
Child does nothing.
Instructor: "Sit on the chair," and gently pushes the child down into the chair.
Instructor: "Well done!"
Instructor: "Sit on the chair."
Child sits on the chair.
Instructor: "Excellent!" and gives the child a small piece of carrot.

To introduce the "under" and "over" concepts, just model these for the child, such as demonstrating a toy going under the chair. As the child repeats the action, say something to the effect of: "Yes, that's good going under the chair."

Then say: "Go under the chair." When the child completes this unaided give them an edible reinforcer.

Sequencing

The child of four is acquiring the necessary skills for sequencing. To help him with this task, present the child with a set of cards that give a small sequence of events, three in a sequence is enough to start with, you can then increase the number to five or more over time. Alternatively, draw the sequences yourself.

Begin by asking: "Tell me what is happening in the pictures." From there introduce some written word cards. These should be large to begin with, and should have the words "first", "then", and "last" written on them. Then, as the child begins to tell you what's happening in the pictures, he can be helped to make sense of them by studying the pictures on the cards.

Example

Sitting at the table, the instructor places three cards in a row in front of the child from left to right in order. The teaching trial goes something like this:

Instructor: "Tell me about the pictures."
Child tells about the pictures.

At this stage the child is liable to leave out a lot of important features from their account and so these should be pointed out by the instructor, such as: "Yes, and look at the boy, he's all dirty, why do you think he's all dirty?" The instructor then goes through the story with the child.

Example

Assume the cards depict a boy walking along a road. The next card has a picture of a car splashing through a puddle and the water going all over the boy. The final card shows the boy all muddy from being splashed.

Instructor: "First," and points to the first picture card, with the boy walking along the road.
Instructor: "Then," and points to the second card, where the boy is being splashed.
Instructor: "Last," and points to the third picture card, where the boy is all muddy from being splashed.
Instructor: "Now you try. First . . ."
Child: "The boy is walking."
Instructor: "Say 'First'."
Child: "First."

44

Instructor: "Good."
Instructor: "First the boy is walking along the road."
Child: "First the boy is walking along the road."
Instructor: "Very well done!"
Instructor: "Where is the boy walking?"
Child: "Along the road."
Instructor: "Splendid, the boy IS walking along the road."

The child can then be released from the teaching trial and the teaching units can be built up over time.

When the child is again presented with the cards, and the procedure is gone through again, this time begin to introduce two cards into the sequence. Run through the first card again, and see how much the child can remember, then go on and introduce the second card as you did for the first. At your next sitting lay out all three cards and run through these from start to finish. So now our child knows what's expected of him and he is already able to do the first two cards independently. Go on to include card three and build up the sequences.

When the child can be presented with all the cards and can tell what's happening in all of them, give him lots of reinforcement. But if the child is getting stuck with the "first", "then", and "last" parts of the statements, try giving him word cards, as this will help him with the correct sequencing.

Example

The instructor places the cards in front of the child and asks him to say, from left to right, what's happening in the cards.

The instructor can help by saying: "First."
Then the child tells what's happening in the first card.
Instructor: "Then."
The child tells what's happening in the second card.
Instructor: "Last."
And the child tells what's happening in the third card.

Remember to begin your reinforcement schedule at the stage when the child is just beginning to say what's in the pictures. Then when he gets the "first" correct, then as he includes this in the sentence. Carry on, incorporating all of the cards into the sequence. The reinforcement should gradually encompass two cards, with the correct wording being used, then all three cards should be spread out in front of the child and the instructor says: "Put them in order." The child then puts the cards in the correct order, and is reinforced for this. Then the child tells the instructor what is happening in the sequence, and again the child is reinforced. The instructor can always help by saying "first", "then", and "last" (or "finally"). Alternatively, the instructor can hand the child the written words on cards, one at a time, as this helps him with the correct ordering.

Eventually this teaching trial should look like this:

The instructor gives the child all three cards and says: "Put in order."

The verbal child should be able tell of the events in the cards as they put them in order.

When the child can do this, with as many as five in the sequence, with the cards being referred to as "first", "next", "then", and "last/finally", then introduce this into the natural environment by having the child tell of sequences in their life such as, "How do we brush our teeth?" or "How do we make a drink?"

The child first relays the sequence of events before being asked to go on and do it.

Defining objects

The defining of objects is a supplementary programme that can help the child with their sequencing. Here cards or objects can be used, the objective being for the child to tell you what an object is for.

Example

The child is shown a cup.
Instructor: "What do we do with it?"
Instructor: "We drink with it."

Instructor: "What do we do with it?"
Child: " We drink with it."
Instructor: "What a star, go outside and play."

An expansion of the categories programme looks something like this:
The child is shown a card with a foodstuff on it and asked:

Instructor: "What is it?"
Instructor: "A biscuit, a biscuit is FOOD."
Instructor: "What is it?"
Child: "Food."
Instructor: "That's right, a biscuit is FOOD, say 'A biscuit is food'."
Child: "A biscuit is food."
Instructor: "You said it," and gives the child a biscuit.

Build your labels up and ask the child to tell you what they are as you
present them to them quickly and at random.

Example

Instructor: "What is it?"
Child: "Orange."
Instructor: "Yes you're quite right, it is an orange, and an
orange is FOOD. What is an orange?"
Child: "Food."
Instructor: "Hurray!" and blows a toy windmill.

Our next teaching trial concerns consequences. i.e. What would happen
if? These programmes are meant to SHOW the child rather than
TELLING him.

Example

Instructor: "What would happen if I pricked the balloon?"
Child says nothing.
Instructor pricks the balloon and it pops. "BANG!"
Instructor: "What happens when I prick the balloon?" and prepares to
prick another.

Child: "Bang."
Instructor pricks the balloon.
Instructor: "BANG."

Similarly, the instructor says: "What would happen if I dropped the egg?"
Child says nothing.
Instructor drops the egg. "SPLAT!"
Then the child is asked to relate what just happened.
Instructor: "The egg broke when I dropped it."
Instructor: "What happened when I dropped the egg? It went splat!"
Instructor: "What happened when I dropped the egg?"
Child: "Splat."
Instructor: "SPLAT!"
The child asks to see the egg splat.
Instructor "Oh, you want to see the egg go splat, do you?"
Child: "Yes."

This is one of those moments when a reinforcer has arisen spontaneously. Seize the moment. Anything that the child was having difficulty with, or that they were giving you a hard time over, ask for this before giving him the egg splat.

Introducing WHY? into our child's vocabulary

Example

The instructor shows the child a picture of a boy crying and standing besides his overturned bicycle.

Instructor: "Why is the boy crying?"
Instructor: "Because he fell off his bike."
Instructor: "Why is the boy crying? Be . . ."
Child: "Because he fell off his bike."

Instructor: "That's right. The boy is cr . . ."
Child: "Crying."

48

Instructor: "Yes, the boy is crying. WHY is he crying?"
Child: "Fell off the bike."
Instructor: "Yes."
Instructor: "Who fell off the bike? The . . . ?" and points to the boy.
Child: "Boy."
Instructor: "You're absolutely right, the boy fell off the bike."
Instructor: "You are wonderful, what are you? Wo . . ."
Child: "Wonderful."
Instructor: "Yes you are wonderful. Come, let's go to the park."

CHAPTER 5

Teaching a five-year-old

By five years of age, children are expected to be able to put on their own clothes, although the tying of shoelaces is, as yet, usually still beyond them. So the child needs to have practice. To do this, have lots of small objects for him to spoon back and forth into containers.

The fastening of buttons is best practiced on a jacket with large buttons. Put the jacket in front of the child so that they can see what they are doing.

Writing

To prepare for this we begin with the holding of the pencil or crayon, use the thick ones to begin with. To start our child off with this, we have them write on a vertical slope.

Whether writing letters, numbers, or shapes, begin by presenting these to the child as dotted lines which can then be traced over. Remember to reinforce the child at all stages, such as when holding the pencil, when holding their wrist in the correct position, for attempting to do the activity, and so on. We can then begin to chain these together as soon as possible: 1. the child picks up the crayon; 2. he is holding his wrist against the board. This is a two-part chain and should be reinforced as such. From here on build up your chain until all of the activity can be done without the child having to be egged on by the reinforcement.

When you have to correct the holding of the pencil, do so without saying anything to the child. If the holding of the instrument proves to be a problem, then wrap a rubber band around the area of grip as this helps to steady a child's hand.

When introducing letters, draw boxes for each individual character in order to address the size of the handwriting.

The method of chaining, as mentioned before, can be used to help the child write his name.

Example

The instructor presents the child with three boxes (for our example of Sam), obviously increase the number depending on your child's name.

Instructor: "Write your name."

Begin with lower case letters. If the child's name is Sam, then in the second and third boxes write "a" and "m", then (HOH) guide the child to write the capital letter "S". This you then reinforce.

On another occasion, we can present the child with three boxes with only the last character filled in, and (HOH) them to fill in the missing letters, followed by reinforcement. The same can be done with only the middle "a" present, and the child has to add the "S" and the final "m", then reinforce.

Eventually you should be able to show the child three blank boxes and say: "Write your name."

To teach the child to draw, take a piece of A4 paper and draw a line down the middle. On one side draw a simple structure such as a large rectangle with a smaller on top, then an even smaller one on top of that, with curly smoke coming out from the top one in the form of a rudimentary boat.

On the other side draw almost everything the same, except for the curly smoke.

The instructor then says: "What's different?" and talks the child through the details of the picture and together they identify the missing smoke. The instructor then reinforces this and proceeds to the next stage. Here the instructor (HOH) guides the child to draw the missing part, the smoke, which is then reinforced—but not too much reinforcement in this case, because the instructor has had to assist the child.

Over a period of time, when the child is being presented with more and more of the missing picture, he is then asked: "Draw the picture." Eventually he will have a small repertoire of things that he can draw, and then he is ready to join other children in this activity.

The skill of colouring has been show above, and can be taught by means of applying clear nail varnish around the items to be coloured, which acts as a barrier and helps the child to stay within the lines.

Gradually introduce shapes. Start by having the child draw around a square card, then draw the three sides of a square, and have the child fill in the missing line to complete the square. All shapes can be approached like this and then the child can colour, cut, and glitter, as well as label them, all part of the process.

Drawing a recognisable body with a head and all limbs is a skill that is usually acquired by the age of five. Helping the child to gain this skill requires patience and practice. Beginning with a model for the child to trace over is far easier than (HOH) and can be backward or forward chained, so that the child must draw the head, with the instructor then drawing in the rest for them to copy over.

The next time you present these to the child, just have the head drawn. The child may protest at this stage as he is used to doing only the head, but whenever this should happen just firmly and gently (HOH) them through the activity, reassuring them rather than reinforcing. (Instructor: "Come on, you can do it." "See, you did it—easy peasy lemon squeezy.")

Show the child's handiwork off to whoever comes in contact with him, and display his efforts on the fridge or a wall—aim to make the child feel proud of his work.

The programme whereby the child copies the instructor is easily applied when doing pencil and paper work, and many skills can be incorporated into this activity.

Example

The instructor and the child sit side by side.

Instructor: "Copy me," and draws a line down the centre of the page, then after the child has done as instructed, the instructor reinforces this, and then asks for a different item, and also changes his/her use of language. So the next thing they ask:

Instructor: "Try this," and draws a horizontal line.
Child complies.
Instructor: "Wow, amazing stuff."
Instructor: "But can you do this?" and draws a cross.
Child almost makes a copy.
Instructor: "Good try."
Instructor: "You try," and repeats the activity.

As the child tries again, help him to be more precise. Get him to draw a vertical line, then a horizontal, then a variety of these, and do them quickly. There is no need for the child to make a perfect cross, just show him the correct formation when you think he is ready, not when he is just starting out. Make sure you model the correct formation of the cross, with the lines more or less bisecting in the middle—often the child is unaware of the importance of this and feels he has done what was requested of him simply by getting the lines to cross at any point.

Toilet training

This need not be a big deal—if your child has an accident don't make a huge issue out of it, just wash and arrange him without mentioning the incident, and remember not to make eye contact with him.

The child should be taken to the toilet every half an hour to begin with, set an alarm if necessary.

Instructor: "It's toilet time."
The child is then taken to the bathroom.

As children on the autistic spectrum are apt to take things literally, please refrain from saying words to the effect of, "Go to the toilet," or "Do the toilet," as this can be confusing for the child—he might respond to "Go to the toilet" by doing just that, going to that room and standing. Well, he did what you asked! And what is meant by "Do the toilet"?

A better strategy is for the instructor to say: "Put your wee wee in the toilet."

The use of a clock is a good idea, as it becomes associated with the inconvenience of having to stop what the child is doing and going to the bathroom, rather than the instructor being the baddy. The time span can be expanded as necessary.

With regard to the self-cleaning process, this is best addressed by using moistened baby wipes, which are far easier for the child to use than dry toilet paper. Be careful not to block the toilet bowl, have a separate, covered bin for disposal of the wipes.

Socialisation

At this stage we shall begin to build on those play skills that we taught to our child when we were introducing them to the concept of friendship.

The friend should be invited to the park or similar space where the children are free to run around. With the adults participating, we are going to introduce your child to the world of competition, chases and races, including egg and spoon races and wheelbarrow races. Have prizes, and rig the game so that your child gets to win often.

The child will at first have to be given the correct language to use, so hold him and cue him to say: "Chase me." When the child says it, everybody chases him. The same applies for hide-and-seek. Have an adult hide with the child, to show him the rules, the same goes for the seeking. The child who is doing the seeking should be encouraged to count aloud, and when the time is right the instructor holds the child and says: "When do you want to go? Say, 'Now'."

Child: "Now."

Instructor: "Now," and lets go of the child. Together, they go and seek. Repeat this until the child says "Now" unaided.

Build up the amount of time spent playing, from five minutes to 20. Try not to let the children become bored, so make sure you have lots of activities planned for them to do.

Critical appraisal

To teach our child the art of criticism, we need a set of cards with things that are wrong in the pictures or draw your own, such as a teapot with the spout upside down, or a teacup with no handle. The child is then asked to identify what's wrong in the picture.

To enhance the skill of observation, have him encounter objects that have been deliberately taken out of context and place where the child will encounter them, for example placing a frozen sausage where his toothbrush is usually kept. This also helps the development of language, as he enquires: "What's that doing there?" or similar. If your child doesn't say this, encourage him to do so.

Example

The child pulls back the covers on his bed and there he finds a broom.

Instructor: "Say 'What's that doing there?'"
Child: "What's that doing there?"

Instructor: "Yes, what's that doing there?" and scratches the child's head.

Now is a good time to introduce the "follow me" programme. Here the child sits on a chair with the instructor in a chair next to them. In front of both is a row of items, two of each, such as two beanbags, two bells, two whistles, and two balls.

The instructor says: "Follow me," and goes through the row of items, throwing, bouncing or blowing, depending on the nature of the item, until they reach the end, where they then do the same thing back along the row of items, until they have again returned to their seat.

The next time the instructor says: "Follow me," and moves one at a time to different objects, and as he does so he (HOH) the child to do the same with their items, all the way back through the sequence, until both are back in their chairs. The instructor then repeats the whole sequence, saying: "Follow me," and nudges the child to get up from their chair to do the same.

Keep the child applied to the task by pointing at the item that he should be copying. The instructor then models the action for the child to copy. If the child begins to wander off halfway through the sequence, gently guide him back.

Reinforce the activities one at a time, then two and so on until the whole sequence is completed, and the reinforcement is only given at the point when the child is back in his chair.

This activity can be included in the play dates when the children are in the park, with a prize being given at the end of the sequence.

Taking turns is to be supervised by the adult present. The playing of musical chairs is good for this, as is I-spy, in fact any game in which a child has to await his turn. Include the child in the discussion as to whose turn it is, as here he can learn to negotiate. Also show him the idea of cheating. For instance, jump in and try to take his turn and have someone say loudly: "Hey that's cheating." "What's he doing?" And everyone says: "Cheating!" You can then show and explain to the child what this means.

Reinforcement should be at the conclusion of the game. Duration of time is what is being sought, so make the rewards extra special, such as 10 minutes on the computer or with their Gameboy or the promise to take them swimming.

Receptive language

Here we introduce the concept of quantity. When our child is confidently passing things to and fro using plastic jugs and spoons, now is the time to draw a thick black line around the centre of the jug to show him where the half-way mark is.

When the child has one jug filled to the top and an empty one, with the black marker showing where the mid-way is, show him how to half-fill the other jug and reinforce the correct action. Children perform well in each other's company, so have two children together doing the activity. This works particularly well with two little ones in a paddling pool with some plastic jugs, then the splashing backwards and forwards of water is not so messy as when it's done in the bath. It's also great fun.

When it's time to come in for snacks, the children can be shown half an apple or orange etc and asked: "What do you want, half the orange, or a whole orange?"

When introducing colours, have five as your target. Use the same format as for the match programme, and the instructor says: "Match the red one," or "Touch the green one," or "Point to the yellow one." Eventually we begin to introduce two items ("Give me the blue and red cards," "Give me the red bus and green car," "Give me all the purple ones").

To begin this programme, have three identical things, two the target colour and one of a different colour. You can then go on and introduce non-identical items, again there should be no more than three items to begin with, and these should all be items the child is familiar with.

Introduce more things in front of him to make it a bit more challenging, until eventually he should be able to match the words of all five colours to the actual colours.

When all this has been completed, extend it into the natural environment, for example "Find something yellow in the room."

Sequencing

The idea of sequencing is again presented to the child, only the terms we shall be using this time are "bigger", "smaller", and "taller", which replace the "first", "then", "last/finally" used previously.

Boxes of breakfast cereal can be used for this, with the child given the instruction: "Put in order." Then the instructor performs the activity, speaking aloud as he does so. Then the items are gone over again, the instructor saying: "This one is bigger," "this one is in the middle," "the smaller one is at the end," etc.

Example

Instructor: "Which one is at the end?"
Child points to the correct object.
Instructor: "Congratulations, that's right."
The instructor then mixes the items.
Instructor: "Now it's your turn, put them in order."

You can then introduce coloured building blocks to further the programme. Taking 15 blocks, the instructor says: "Do this," and builds a small structure for the child to copy.

Non-verbal assistance is usually all that is necessary if the child puts a wrong-coloured block on the structure—pointing to or tapping the wrong item is usually all that is necessary for the child to rectify this. If the blocks are wrong for any other reason, start again and this time say to the child: "Copy me," and, block by block, the child is guided to imitate the instructor.

It's a good idea to take pictures of ready-made structures which the child can then copy and play with the blocks if he is on his own.

Places

For receptive language, we shall introduce a visual display for the child to use. For this you need a strip of Perspex, about two inches wide and four inches long, on to which are stuck three squares of Velcro, each measuring 3cm. We then laminate three small pictures of places that the child might visit, such as the park, shop or swings. Now we present the visual display to the child.

Instructor: "Where are we going?" and points to the image of the park.
Instructor: "We're going to the park."

Instructor: "Show me where we're going," and (HOH) guides the child to the correct picture.
Instructor: "Yes, that's the one, we're going to the park."

Then the instructor takes to child to the park. On arrival, the instructor asks the child:

Instructor: "Where are we?" and again presents the visual display for the child to point at.

Likewise the child should be presented with the display on arrival back home, although this time he is asked:

Instructor: "Where did we go?"
Child points to the correct picture.
Instructor: "Fantastic."

Expressive language

We are now going to introduce a "describing" programme. To do this we require a set of cards or drawings of different things; a lion, an owl, an apple, and a telephone, for instance.

We begin with one card and ask the child:

Instructor: "What is it?" or "What does it say?" or "Where do we find it?" or "What do we do with it?"

If our first card shows an apple, the instructor says:

Instructor: "Tell me about this."
Instructor: "It's an apple, it's red, it grows on trees, and you eat it."
Instructor: "Tell me about this," and points to the card.
Child: "Apple."
Instructor: "Apple, that's right."
Instructor: "What do we do with an apple?"
Instructor: "We eat it. What do we do with an apple?"
Child: "We eat it."

Instructor: "We eat it, correct."
Instructor: "Tell me something about this," and points to the apple.
Instructor: "It's an apple and we eat it."
Instructor: "It's an . . ."
Child: "Apple."
Instructor: "And we e . . ."
Child: "Eat it."
Instructor: "Yes, it's an apple and we eat it. Brilliant, you can go and play," and let's the child go from the table.

At the next sitting, begin by testing what has already been taught before. If the child remembers, then proceed to the next stage, in which the child tells us three things about an item.

When this card is known, introduce a second. You do this exactly as shown before for the "apple" exercise. Extend this to three or more cards, depending on your child's ability at this stage. Eventually the child will be asked to tell about cards that have been presented randomly.

This programme is then taken into the natural environment. When we show our child a cup, we can then ask him to tell us something about it; its name (cup), feature (made from china), function (you drink from it), etc. Eventually an array of objects can be presented to the child for him to tell us a variety of things about them. The instructor should eventually be able to point out things in the natural environment and say: "Look, there's a bicycle. What do we do with a bicycle?"

The next stage in this programme is for the child to tell you something about people.

Instructor: "Tell me about daddy."
Instructor: "Daddy is tall, has brown hair, and wears glasses."

Then, with other people, have the child tell you what's different about them or what's the same. Try to encourage the child to use adjectives when doing this programme.

The describing programme is then extended to include quantity, so here the child has to describe a thing using the terms "empty" and "full".

To begin this, have two identical drinking glasses, one full and one empty, then ask:

Instructor: "Which one is empty?"
Child touches the empty one.
Instructor: "Which one is full?"
Child touches the full one.
Instructor: "Excellent."

Then encourage the child to use language rather than simply pointing:

Instructor: "Which one is full?"
Child touches the full one.
Instructor: "Correct, this one is full."
Instructor: "Then this one must be e . . ."
Child: "Empty."
Instructor: "Perfect," and tickles the child.
Instructor: "If this one is empty, then this one is . . . ?"
Child: "Empty."
Instructor "Good try."
Instructor: "Touch the empty one."
Child tries to touch the full one.
The instructor blocks this movement so that the child touches the correct item.
Instructor: "That's the empty one."
Instructor: "So this is the f . . ."
Child: "Full one."
Instructor: "Good."
Instructor: "Touch the full one and then the empty one."
The child touches the correct items in the correct order.
Instructor: "That was so good. You can go and bounce on the trampoline."

This exercise should be continued until the child is giving the correct name for both items.

If the child stops answering, then ask him to touch the requested item. If he refuses this, ask him to do some gross motor skills such as touching his head, turning around, clapping, and jumping. Present these actions as quickly as possible and then ask for your target. Always take the child back a step if they stop responding.

Reading

For expressive language with regard to reading, we can use our Perspex visual display for short sequences of events. It will show three icons which tell a story. The sequences can be anything from; going to bed, eating dinner, and putting our shoes on. You can be really creative here, devising all manner of sequences for your child to tell you about.

CHAPTER 6
Teaching a six-year-old

In this chapter we begin with the perceptual motor skills aimed at the six-year-old child. The hop is such a skill. To achieve this we will build on the skills that have already been taught to our child, such as standing on one leg.

To begin this exercise, have the child stand on one leg, with the other leg bent backwards at the knee, with the front of the foot resting on a small stool. He remains in this position as the instructor counts out loud up to five, the instructor then reinforces this action and over time the period spent with the foot resting on the stool is prolonged. This action is then prolonged until the child can hold the stance for a count of 20 seconds.

Eventually the child will have the stool for less and less time until they can hold this movement unaided, when the stool can be finally removed.

Next we begin to build on the time spent holding the movement. The reinforcement schedule should be exactly as for the foot up on the stool, i.e., one, building to five seconds. If the child can only manage two seconds to begin with, then so be it. Eventually he will be able to hold the movement unaided for longer periods. Highly reinforce the child for each episode and prolong the reinforcement after each new target is achieved.

If the child wobbles or falls down then reduce the time required for him to hold the position, regardless of the original target. From there, begin to increase the time according to our child's ability.

When he can stand firmly for at least 15 to 20 seconds, take him by the upper arms and bounce him up and down, as in a hopping movement. Two bounces suffice to begin with, reinforce this and let the child go. From here we can begin to increase the number of independent bounces. When the child is fully engaged he is often unaware that he is doing the movement unaided, and will probably only fall down if he is reminded of his independence. Try to make sure that you're reinforcing all the independent actions, whether the child is aware of this or not. Reinforcing this activity with time spent on a small trampoline is a good idea, since this is a similar action to the one that we are teaching our child.

For outdoor activities and to make this skill fun, try hopping races, hopping into a row of hoops, hopping and then jumping, and set up competitions to see who can hop the longest. Keep the hoops close to each other to begin with—only when hopping in them is mastered should they be moved farther apart. Also remember to ensure that the child is proficient in any skill before establishing an element of competition.

Alternatively, adults can join in the game and rig the outcome so that the child is the winner—hopefully the concept of winning will also gradually filter through to the child.

A row of plastic hoops can also be used for the children to jump in to, with the aim of both feet landing on the ground simultaneously (no stepping). Jumping in and out with both feet landing together without pausing is the next stage, and from there we can progress to three jumps without a pause in between, and so on.

When this is accomplished we progress to hopping from hoop to hoop. Praise the child for each leap then hold back on the praise until two hoops are achieved without pausing, and so on until the child can jump or hop into all of the hoops without pausing.

Writing his name

This is something that we should be constantly working on with our child. Try using magnetic letters for varying the way in which you present the characters to the child.

We began the writing process with individual spaces to show us where the individual letters should be. If the child's writing is too large to begin with, we can write the letters in boxes to help limit the size of the handwriting.

Work through the alphabet, with each letter being presented in dots for the child to join up or magnetic letters for him to trace around.

Eventually the child is shown how to trace each letter with his finger. To encourage this skill—and to ensure that he is having fun—sit the child in front of a sand-filled tray in which he can trace the letters. Alternatively, use shaving foam to add a new twist to the activity as this helps to keep the child motivated.

If the child does not use the material appropriately then remove the materials after one verbal warning. If, for example, he scatters the sand rather than writes in it, then he must clean up the mess, (HOH) if need be. A brush and shovel light enough for the child to work with should be made available. The instructor should say: "Clean it up," and (HOH) they help the child to clean up the mess, with no eye contact or additional language.

This (HOH) should only be at the beginning of the cleaning up process, the child is expected to finish the job on his own lest the task becomes reinforcing of itself (it might be that the child is seeking a lot of attention from the instructor and is achieving just that by making a mess, or alternatively he might be seeking to avoid doing the original task). This is something to watch out for.

The child's grip on a pencil will improve with practice and the techniques that will help with this are, as mentioned before: writing on a slanted board while holding the wrist down on the writing surface; wrist-strengthening exercises such as holding the hands together as in a prayer motion and pressing the palms together; pulling apart some Theraputty; and retrieving marbles from it. These are all good for strengthening the child's hands and wrists.

If you find that Theraputty is too expensive for your budget, any old Playdoh will do—I emphasise OLD, as the older the material is the harder it becomes and therefore the child's hands have to work harder to manipulate it.

Working with shapes: the triangle

The shape we shall be most concerned with for this age group is the triangle. Begin with the child copying a triangle when seated beside you as you model the shape for your child to copy.

The instructions given should, as always, vary as soon as possible.

Example

Instructor: "Copy this."
Instructor: "Can you do this?"
Instructor: "Now you try."

Help the child to cut out, and stick on, triangular forms of differing size and shape.

At this stage begin to help the child to use a ruler to draw the triangle. Model then reinforce the correct holding of the instrument.

We can also show our child how to use an eraser to rub out mistakes when attempting to draw triangles. (HOH) these activities to begin with, for instance showing the child the correct angle at which to hold the eraser. We can then faintly draw a line for the child to rub out.

Have the child write his name at the bottom of all the activities he has completed—if a mistake occurs, as is bound to happen, ask him to rub out the mistake and begin again.

One problem that frequently occurs during this activity is that the child insists on rubbing out all the written words rather than the individual mistake. If this should happen, stop the child from rubbing out the words by blocking the words that are correct with your finger and, if necessary, (HOH) guide the child to write the missing letter, reinforce, then continue with the activity.

This might develop into a battle of wills. However, the child cannot be allowed to enforce his will, since it might establish compulsive behaviour, such as erasing everything instead of the one small error.

This would be a hindrance for the child in the school setting when timing and completion are important factors, so try to work through any maladaptive behaviour by means of (HOH) if necessary, and reinforce the completion of any independent activity.

For example, if the child has made a huge fuss because he has written a single word wrong and insists on rubbing out a whole paragraph, then the instructor should cover the words that are correct and (HOH) lead the child to the wrong word and (HOH) together they rub this word out. The child may be making such a fuss that it takes a lot of energy to keep him on task—that's fine, just exert more force than the child and refrain from looking or talking to him, and as soon as the task is complete reinforce this, then continue the exercise. Do not allow the child to leave the teaching environment at this stage, instead have him write one thing independently, even if it's a single letter.

If the child is still protesting you can say: "You can go, but first you must write the next letter." If the child refuses, then again (HOH) and complete the next letter with him. In this instance the child has not complied with our instruction and so he is required to continue.

In the worst-case scenario should occur, and the child point blank refuses, then (HOH) and keep going! Only when you feel the child's resistance letting up should you start to ease off the guidance, and as they write anything that is appropriate, even one letter! Reinforce, and only then can they be released from the teaching environment.

At a later stage, whenever you think the time is right, try the exercise again. So, for instance, if the child is geared up for a much-wanted outing, or for a ride on his scooter—whatever and whenever—seize the moment and make this longed-for activity obtainable ONLY on condition that he performs the required task again.

It's not necessary to have the exact task set before him again, as winning battles is not the object here—the objective is for the child to comply and for a reduction in the obsessive behaviour. The writing of a sentence rather than the single word should suffice. Believe me, in moments like this you just keep pushing until you squeeze as much as you can from your child, striking while the iron is hot.

Reinforcement should be applied as he begins the task, as he continues, and, of course, at the completion of the task. Then he gets to do the longed-for activity.

How do you know when to stop squeezing? When the child's slight whimpering turns into wriggling about. At this point begin to remind him what he was working to achieve and you only ease off the pressure just as he is about to cave in and throw a wobbly.

But what happens if the child is still not impressed? (HOH) is the order of the day for tasks that are seemingly impossible. It might help to begin the activity at a time in the day when naturally occurring reinforcers such as hunger and thirst—shown to be the most highly motivating reinforcers of all—begin to stir within the child. Try to sip some orange juice, saying "Mmmm" and have the child's glass of juice in full view but out of reach. Say: "You want your juice? Well hurry up then and you can have it." Try to make this sound natural, not something on condition that he performs the task or as though you are bored. Remember the golden rules: do not give in, do not give up.

I have no doubt that you can do this. In the example above, you just helped change your child's cognitive structure. What's that? Just a big way of saying that you made him an offer he couldn't refuse. You changed his mind for him!

Back to the writing, it seems that not correcting mistakes in a negative manner is the way forward. For instance, if the child writes letters back to front, as often happens at this stage of development, show him the correct way by means of modelling (draw an S in the sand and say: "This is how we draw an S").

How writing impacts on the child's world is also important, so encourage him to want to write—have him help you with writing the weekly grocery list, and he can include a request of his own on the list as a treat. Also encourage the writing of thank-you notes and birthday cards etc.

Extending colouring skills

At this stage we need to practice colouring skills. To do this we begin by presenting our child with two thick lines that they have to colour in between.

If you have found that clear nail varnish (to help with the outline, as discussed earlier) is too slow in drying or just plain ineffective, then try paper glue. Alternatively you could run two lines of glue across the page and have the child sprinkle glitter along these—when they are dry they form a barrier to help the child to colour between the lines. As ever, be prepared and have lots of variations of these glitter lines; horizontal, vertical, triangular, and so on.

Ball skills

Start with a game of catch when polishing your child's ball skills. Begin with him sitting very close in front of the instructor (this will be extended over time). A medium-sized ball is preferable, no smaller than a tennis ball, and make sure it's soft enough to avoid injury.

Example

Instructor: "Catch," and drops the ball into the child's cupped hands from close distance. Model the child's hand position and reinforce him for holding that position.

The child might move his hands away before the instructor has a chance to drop the ball into him. To correct this, have someone behind the child who holds the child's hands in the cupped position. When the ball is dropped (not thrown at this stage), the child can be aided in the catching of the ball, then reinforce this.

Once this is mastered, remember to include more ball skills, including throwing under-arm and over-arm, (HOH) these, then catching, and throwing against a wall, patting, also rolling. The logical progression is to bat and ball games, skittles etc.

From catch, try "bounce and catch". Here, the child is positioned holding the ball, with both hands holding the ball at waist level, which you reinforce and from here (HOH) the child to bounce the ball and as it bounces back up (HOH) him to catch it, followed by more reinforcement.

The positioning of the hands should be the first thing you reinforce, then (HOH) bounce the ball together and reinforce, then when the ball bounces back up again (HOH) the child to catch it; reinforce him again.

Try modelling this for the child and show him how many times it's possible for him to bounce and catch the ball—this usually inspires a child to make an extra effort.

When he can bounce and catch the ball independently at least three times, you can then show him how high the ball can be bounced before catching it.

This is best taught last, as children tend to rush into this activity before mastering the first and only want to bounce the ball as high as they can. You might find it difficult to keep him on task because of this.

If this should occur, try using the high bounce as your reinforcer. If this doesn't work, do not allow him access to the ball until they promise to conform—if they say they will and then don't, just stop the activity and with no eye contact or language take him indoors and re-direct him to something else. You can then try the ball games as a reinforcer for something else.

Patting the ball is best done with both hands to begin with, as this makes success more obtainable for the child. Using a Swiss exercise ball for this skill is useful and varies the task for him, as well as being more manageable due to its size.

When the child has mastered these skills, introduce doing and saying at the same time. Have the child singing the alphabet, the days of the week, saying rhyming words, or even saying their times tables as they pat the ball at the same time.

Socialisation

For our six-year-old, we shall begin with teaching him the greeting response.

As people arrive at the house, ask him to greet the child, who must then look at the person who is greeting him and say hello.

The instructor begins by asking for eye contact, saying: "Look at me," and gently holding the child's chin so that he is looking at the instructor.

Sometimes the child still avoids eye contact. If this is so, hold up a small reinforcer in front of the child, then pull it towards you up to eye level, as this acts as an incentive for the child to look towards the instructor's eyes. Immediately reinforce this, praise the child and give him a piece of the reinforcer that you held up.

A "look at me" programme can be devised for the child, who then receives reinforcement every time he looks at the instructor, who withholds any interaction until eye contact is made, however brief. This skill is one where firmness is imperative, as this splitting off from the interaction is what will make the child stand out and seem odd to other children, who may then become reluctant to interact with him because of this.

A helpful thing when interacting with your child is to always bring him towards you before talking to him. Many times parents will address their child from across a busy room, where there are conversations taking place and the TV is on. Try not to do this, as it puts our child at a disadvantage—the chances of him filtering out this additional information in order to respond to you is hindered.

Remember to limit your use of language when asking "look at me".

Example

Instructor: "Look at me."
Child ignores the instruction.
Instructor: "Look at me," and takes the child's chin in their hand.

Child looks briefly at the instructor.

Instructor: "Good," and this should be followed through with the next trial, as quickly as possible.

Instructor: "Look at me," and holds a biscuit in front of their face for the child to focus on.

Child looks at the biscuit.

Instructor: "Good looking," and raises the biscuit so that the child's eyes meets theirs.

Instructor: "Magic."

Our target now is for the child to sustain eye contact for longer periods of time:

Instructor: "Look at me."

Child looks at the instructor.

Instructor: "Fantastic," and quickly follows on from this with a piece of the biscuit.

When the child responds to "Look at me" without the reinforcer being held up for him to follow, he receives a larger piece of the biscuit. If the eye contact is sustained for five or more seconds, more of the biscuit can be given.

When the next teaching time begins, after the initial praise for some other known response (such as "Come here,") which sets the child up on a winning streak, we can then ask:

Instructor: "Look at me," and gauge how much our child has retained from the previous teaching trial. In time the "look at me" instruction will be completely phased out, and we can then reinforce any spontaneous looking.

Group work

We are now ready to introduce our six-year-old to group work, with the main objective of increasing his awareness of others and his environment.

We start by assembling four children together who are at varying stages in ability, although they should all be of similar age. The gatherings should preferably be on a weekly basis and for about 30 minutes.

Begin by introducing the children to each other while they are sitting in a circle. From here onwards we are training our child in social skills, such as; how to behave in a group, how to deal with distractions, learning to work through ideas within a group context, eye contact, listening, taking turns, and asking questions. We are also looking to expand our child's range of interests.

Example

Instructor: "Hello, my name is . . ."

The instructor then looks at the next person in the circle (our child) and instructs:

Instructor: "Say, 'Hello my name is . . .'."
Child: "Hello, my name is Eden."

After saying his name the child is discreetly reinforced (for example, a discreet whisper saying: "Well said, Eden.").
The instructor then looks to the next child in the circle:

Instructor: "Your turn."

If necessary help this child as well, and so on, until all the children have been introduced. From here we begin to assemble some group rules. Examples of these are; we always put our hand up when we want to speak, we don't talk when someone else is talking, we listen to others, and we sit nicely in our seats etc.

The sessions should focus on one particular skill at a time, such as; greetings, making friends, eye contact, listening, observation, and turn-taking. The instructor should monitor these skills in order to judge which are necessary to develop the following week. Weekly sessions, conducted at a regular time, are advisable as this helps the children to structure their world.

We can then move on to games for the children to play, such as the "What's different?" game. For this we have one of the children leave the room and an assistant helps him to alter his appearance. This should be easy and quick to do, for instance rolling up one or both of their sleeves or trouser legs, letting down a girl's long hair, and putting on a jumper back to front or inside out.

The child returns to the room and the others are asked: "What's different?"

Eventually, the aim is for the group to give more information about themselves ("I have blue eyes," "I have a big sister," "I am six," "I went to the cinema.") with the intention of encouraging our child to listen and ask questions spontaneously. To do this we may need to give him the first question, then when he asks it he gets a really special reinforcer. Then when he realises that all he has to do to get a special treat is to ask a question, he will begin to make the effort.

Of course, special reinforcers are rather rare, so to ensure that they retain their reinforcing value, begin to put in place what is referred to as a "token system". This is something that can contain five or more tokens and when the child collects them all that extra-special reinforcer is theirs.

Examples of a token system can be a jar to which you add a marble into every time the child does what is expected of him, or a sticker chart where the child gets a sticker every time he gets closer to his goal.

Activities

Eventually the group will have a small repertoire of activities that they can play together. Try to have some assignments that require paper and pencil and then you can give him a short worksheet, which contains three things (this is all that is necessary to begin with).

Example

1. What I like about myself.
2. What I don't like about myself.
3. One thing I would like to change about myself.

Also try having a group discussion on how we communicate, such as the definition of body language and its role (e.g. tone of voice, eye contact, body orientation, and how the group rate themselves on each of these skills). Role playing and working in pairs is good for this.

Another discussion can centre on the nature of assertiveness (expressing feelings, standing up for yourself, making requests and/or suggestions, refusing, disagreeing, apologising, complaining). The overall aim here is for the group to grasp the essentials of communicating their wants and needs.

You might also like to try an activity centred on observation. What does our group look like? Hair, is it curly, straight, long, or short? Eye colour? Height? How do we communicate (in terms of volume, clarity, rate, fluency, and intonation)? How do we feel when people ignore us, won't be friends with us, or shout at us?

If any of the group breaks the communication rules, such as not putting up their hand before asking a question or talking over another group member, these things should be put on extinction (i.e. ignored) and reinforced when adhered to.

Games

Pass the parcel can be added to your list, because it is and excellent way to teach turn-taking and waiting. Musical chairs is another, in fact almost all games played at children's parties are suitable, and they have the advantage that most children will already be familiar with him.

For a memory game, have a tray of objects and show these to the children, then cover him with a tea towel and the children have to remember as many as they can.

All the children should be given a tangible reinforcer for attending the group, in order to encourage him to want to come back.

Some homework for instructors

The following section is for our instructor to work on outside of group time.

The art of conversation

For this to occur, our child must learn to ask questions and to make comments. The instructor must also make comments for our child to ask questions about. Try to avoid making the process seem like you are drilling the child, as he will not find this reinforcing.

Make two cards, one with the word "Comment" on it and the other saying "Question".

Example

I went to the zoo. (Comment)
What did you see? (Question)

The instructor then makes a comment or asks a question:

Instructor: "I went to the park yesterday."
The child then chooses whether to ask a question or make a comment. This they indicate by means of pointing to the "Question" or "Comment" card.
Child: "What did you do?"

Reinforce this as naturally as possible at this stage—if the child gets stuck, give him the language as he would say it. Alternatively, the child can pick a pre-written card that has a comment or question on it, which he reads aloud. If possible, start with the verbal task first, because the cards have to be phased out eventually.

Example

Instructor: "Say, 'I kicked the leaves'."
Child: "I kicked the leaves."
Instructor: "Kicked the leaves! That sounds like fun."
Instructor: "What else did you do at the park?"
Child: "I went on the swing."
Instructor: "I want to kick leaves and go on the swing. Let's go to the park," and they go to the park.

A high level of reinforcement (the park) is given for this independent use of language, but have a good selection of different responses that do not stray too far from the theme.

Observation and language

For the "I See" game we place two objects in front of our child, for example a toy frog and a toy duck. These are then added to, depending on how quickly the child manages to do the exercise.

The instructor (HOH) guides the child to touch first the frog and then the duck, while saying;

Instructor: "I see a frog and a duck, what do you see?"
Instructor: "I see a frog and a d . . ."
Child: "Duck."
Instructor: "Yes, it's a duck!"

The instructor repeats this segment until:

Child: "I see a frog and a duck," when asked "What do you see?"

The next stage is to increase the amount of items we set before the child, up to five. The instructor will need to model the language for the child:

Instructor: "I see a frog, a duck, AND a car."

When the child says "AND", reinforce him at this point in the sentence, as well as at the beginning and at the end of the list of items. Do this for all the items, remembering to vary the way that you reinforce your child. The exchange should go something like this:

Example

Child: "I . . ."
Instructor: "Yes."
Child: ". . . see a frog, a duck, a car, a sweet, and . . ."
Instructor: "Good."
Child ". . . a ball."
Instructor: "Terrific! You remembered all of him."
At the next trial, the instructor says "Good" at the same point (reinforcing "AND") only more softly. The next time, he can remove the reinforcement of "AND" altogether, replacing it with an obvious

nod of the head, or a smile—another example of how to differentially reinforce the child.

Receptive language

We can now commence number work with our child, starting with adding and subtracting numbers up to five and beginning with the number one.

Using an Etch-a-Sketch or a chalkboard (although almost anything you can write on will suffice, because varying the way that the information is presented to our child helps to keep him motivated), the instructor begins: "One plus one is?" "One plus two is?" "One plus three is?" and "One plus four is?"

It is usually helpful to give the child a visual clue, and for this you can use the counters from a tiddly-winks set, or larger if possible. So, when we ask our child what one plus four makes, if he is unsure of the answer we can help him by giving him the counters to work it out with.

Example

The instructor gives the child one of the counters and asks him to make four. The instructor then (HOH) helps him to put the other counters with this one to make up the number four.

Start with a row of counters spread out in front of the child, give him one of them and ask him to make whatever number you requested. The child then has to put the other counters with this one to give the answer—it helps if at first you count aloud with him.

When the child is proficient in these we progress to simple counting. For this you'll need some blank postcards and a two pence piece with which to draw circles on the cards.

Draw one circle in the middle of one of the postcards, then two circles on another and so on until you have five postcards all with circles on them varying from one to 10. Then colour in all the circles.

The instructor and child begin sitting side by side at the table and the instructor helps him to count by using the counters (or two-pence pieces if you've had difficulty finding counters of a suitable size) and the cards.

Example

The instructor puts down the card with one circle on it and below this places a two pence piece.

Instructor: "Count one," and lifts the two pence piece and puts it on the "one" circle.
Instructor: "Count one," and (HOH) helps the child to lift the coin on to the circle in the card.
Instructor "Good stuff."
Instructor: "Count one," and points to the coin.
Child lifts the coin.
Instructor: "Good trying."
Instructor: "Count one," and points to the circle.
Child picks up the two pence coin and places it in the circle.
Instructor: "Excellent!" and gives the child a small reinforcer for a couple of minutes.

Now that our child is familiar with what's expected of him we can begin to build up the number of cards that he can correctly place counters on (follow the example above, working through all the cards).

We can then place two coins below our number one card and ask: "Count one."

Now the child is learning to count. The amount of coins in this instance should be greater than the sum requested, so for "Count two" we have three or more coins available for the child to choose from.

When he has successfully been taught the correct answers we can then place two cards in front of him, the task being to identify the correct card. The coins in this case will not exceed the larger target, so when two cards are put in front of the child, one has three circles on it, and the other has one circle on it. Then the instructor says: "Count one," and gives the child three coins.

It's still a bit of a giveaway, as the child has the same amount of coins in his hand as there are circles on the higher card. This will gradually change, however, as the child begins to make progress and we give him an even larger amount of coins, these will then be larger in sum than both numbers on the cards.

For example, we give the child two cards, one with four circles on it and another with two circles. We then give our child seven counters and ask him to count two, or count four.

Sometimes the child assumes that we are asking him to put counters on all the available circles. If this happens, just gently block him from doing so by moving his hand away as he attempts to put the remaining counters on all the circles, then quickly reinforce the first response (when the first correct number of coins have been placed on the correct circles), ignoring the wrong movement as you block it.

The next stage of counting uses two sets of number cards, which go up to 20. The instructor and child each have a set, then the instructor puts down a card and says: "I will tell you a number and you have to tell me the partner that will make the number."

The instructor then says the number 12 and puts down the card number one and (HOH) the child choses from his pile of cards the number two card. This is then placed alongside the number one card to create the number 12. Remember to increase your level of reinforcement for any unaided response.

Body parts revisited

Ask your child to point out these parts or sections of the body, in order of feet to hair; mouth, eyes, nose, feet, hair, tongue, head, ears, hands, legs, arms, fingers, stomach, back, teeth, toes, chin, thumbs, knees, neck, fingernails, heel, ankle, jaw, chest, wrist, shoulder, hip, elbow, and waist.

Time concepts

These include the seasons as well as the time of day and can be taught in the natural environment (for winter, the child and instructor can make a snowman and then make a picture of the snowman using cotton wool balls and glitter, while autumn involves collecting fallen leaves, painting them and sticking them on to paper to create a collage).

We can then have a collection of pictures, or the real items, set out in front of the child and be able to say: "When do we wear these?" while pointing to a pair of sunglasses. Eventually we should be able to transfer these to the natural environment and our child should easily be able to respond with "Umbrella" or "Raincoat if we ask: "It's raining, what do we need?"

To ensure that this concept is driven home, reverse the way in which you ask it.

Example

Instructor: "It's raining, what do we need?"
Child: "Umbrella."
Instructor: "Umbrella. We use an umbrella when it's r . . ."
Child: "Raining."
Instructor: "Raining, we use our umbrella when it's raining."

The child will eventually be expected to go and get the item. Alternatively we can have two objects, and say: "It's a rainy day, which do we need, sunglasses or Wellingtons?" Or with three or more items, say: "Which of these do we use when we go to the seaside?"

Eventually we move on to what comes first, spring or summer? Or what comes after summer? Try to present these questions in as many different ways as you can think of.

More complex items

As the list of items that our six-year-old can recognise expands, we need to ensure that our child becomes familiar with more complex items such as an acorn, a flask, thorn, compass, needle and thread, and a choir. Gradually add these examples, and more, to your list.

Listening skills

To ensure that our child is listening well we will set up some tasks for him to complete. To begin with we give our child some instructions, which he must follow through in the correct order. The instructions should be fairly simple to begin with and should be compiled from things that he is already familiar with.

If the child is struggling to retain the information, simply reduce the number of things on the list.

Example

Stand up, clap, and turn around.
Wave, touch your nose, and sit down.
Go to the door, turn around, and jump.
Touch your nose, clap, and find something in the room that is red.
Go to the bench, sit down, and put your hands on your head.

Listening comprehension

For this aspect of listening we can use spoken or written material. Written material is the far easier of the two, because the child has something in front of him that he can refer to.

Begin with two or three sentences and have the child follow as you read aloud to him. We are looking at the child's inference skills here, so he must do more than simply repeat the information.

Example

Instructor: "Camels live in the desert."
Instructor: "Where would we find a camel?"

Here the instructor has avoided asking the obvious question, "Where do camels live", and by so doing has forced the child to re-phrase the information. Expand on this as much as possible so that the child has to really think about the information.

We can then move on to having the child read something aloud and the instructor asking him questions about it. This is a good way of finding out whether your child has retained the information that he has just heard, merely by asking him what you just said.

Expressive language

This lesson concentrates on comparatives and superlatives.

Example

We begin by having three boxes, in ascending order, set out in front of the child. The instructor, (HOH) with the child, touches the smaller of the boxes and says "Big", then touching the next box says "Bigger". On touching the third box, he says, "Biggest".

Instructor: "Now you try."

Child (HOH) touches the boxes as before, only this time the instruction looks something like this:

Instructor: "B . . ."
Child: "Big."
Instructor: "Big, that's the one."

The Instructor then moves on to the next box and again (HOH) helps the child.

Instructor: "Bigger."
Instructor: "Say, 'Bigger'."
Child: "Bigger."
Instructor: "Bigger, well done."

The instructor then moves on to the third box, and again (HOH) with the child touches this box and says:

Instructor: "Biggest."
Child: "Biggest."
Instructor: "Hey, that was amazing!" and gives the child a small piece of fruit.

Eventually the child will be able say what the next two items are, after being given only the first one as a cue.

Example

Instructor: "If this one is Big, then this one is B . . . ?" and points to the next item in the row.

Child: "Bigger."
Instructor: "Fantastic!"
Instructor: "And so this one must be the B . . ." and points to the third, biggest, box.
Child: "Biggest."
Instructor: "That was incredible!"

Eventually present these in different orders, for example:

Instructor: "Big, bigger and b . . ."
Child: "Biggest."

The reasoning behind this is that our child does not just repeat big, bigger, and biggest without truly understanding the concept.

When the instructor is able to ask the child to point to the bigger box or the biggest box, the child is ready to move on to:

Instructor: "Put these in order, beginning with Big."

Using the same method, we can begin to teach our child concepts such as tall, short, near, further away, closest, and so on. When our child is familiar with the above information we can then ask him to use his own words and tell us: "Which one is tall?" or "Which is taller?"

For this to happen, we may have to guide him in the correct use of language.

Example

Instructor: "Which one is taller?"
Instructor: "This one is taller," and points to the taller item.
Instructor: "Which one is taller?"
Instructor: "Say, 'This one is taller'," and touches the taller item.
Child: "This one is taller," and points to the correct item.
Instructor: "Superb!"
Instructor: "Which one is taller?"
Child touches the taller item.
Instructor: "Say, 'This one is taller'."
Child: "This one is taller."

Instructor: "Excellent!" Give me a high-five.
Child complies.
Instructor: "Can you touch the taller?"
Child touches the taller one.
Instructor: "Perfect," and tickles the child.

Story comprehension

For a story to have meaning for our child, it's best to begin with him as its main character. Begin with simple sentences such as: "Eden went to the park." Then ask: "Who went to the park?" or "Where did Eden go?"

For the next stage you'll need two pictures, one of the park and of your child. Start with two blank cards, preferably the same size as playing cards, and write on them "WHERE?" and "WHO?" before explaining to the child what those words say and what is happening in the pictures. This last might seem self-explanatory, but many a programme has been hindered by an instructor asking for the park while another instructor has been asking for the garden—for the same picture.

The instructions look something like this:

Instructor: "What does it say?" and shows the child the card in question.
Instructor: "Where is it?" and points to the place shown in the picture.
The instructor then sits with the picture of the park on the table in front of the child and hands the "WHERE?" card to the child:

Instructor: "Where does it go?" and puts the word card with the picture.
Instructor: "That's where it goes."
Instructor: "Where does it go?" and (HOH) guides the child to place the word card with the correct picture.
Instructor: "Very well done!"
Instructor: "Where does it go?" and hands the card to the child.
Child does nothing.
Instructor: "Where does it go?" and points to the picture.
Child does nothing.
The instructor nudges the child's arm while looking at the corresponding picture.

Child puts the word card with the correct picture.
Instructor: "Hooray."

When the child has mastered this stage, put two pictures in front of him and hand him one of the word cards. You can vary this by using two word cards and one of the pictures.

Example

Instructor: "Match WHO," and guides the child to the picture of himself.

As always, begin by asking the child to follow the instruction before attempting to (HOH) him, just to make sure you're not underestimating his ability. Then if necessary (HOH) the child to put the correct card with the corresponding picture. The (HOH) guidance should gradually transform into this order; first physical, then gesturing, and finally verbal.

Plurals

To teach this we begin with 3D objects, as well as 2D cards. Put three marbles together and have a single marble set off to the side. Then point to the single marble and say "One marble". Then point to the three marbles and say "Many marbles" with emphasis on the "S" at the end, making sure that he can clearly hear the emphasis. Then ask him to give you the marbleS or the marble.

When using 2D cards, have pictures showing one child and some showing several children, and say: "Point to the girl," or "Where are the boys?" Expand on your use of vocabulary at this stage by asking the child for a few, some, and a couple etc, after having first demonstrated these for him.

Irregular plurals

This term refers to those quirks of our language which frustrate all those learning English as a second language. Irregular plurals include such things as; mice/mouse, people/person, sheep/sheep, child/children, man/men, and so on.

To address this issue we simply need to give our child some gentle exposure to these things.

Example

Place two pictures, drawn by you or cut from old magazines, and sit by the child with both pictures on the table in front of him. Pointing at the cards, the instructor gives the names of the objects depicted.

Instructor: "Man," and points to the picture of the man.
Instructor: "Men," and points to the picture showing more than one man.
Instructor: "Now you try, point to the men."
Child points to the men.
Instructor: "Very well done."
Instructor: "Point to the man," and points to the man.
Child ignores the instruction.
Instructor: "Show me pointing."
Child complies.
Instructor: "That's nice pointing."
Instructor: "Point to the man."
Child complies.
Instructor: "Super duper, well done."
Instructor: "Point to the men," and points at the men.
Child complies.
Instructor: "Thank you, that was very good pointing."
The Instructor then changes the position of the cards.
Instructor: "Which do you want?" and holds up a car and a toy frog.
Child reaches for the frog.
Instructor: "Good," and squeezes the frog, its eyes pop out.
Child giggles.
Instructor: "Do you want the frog?"
Child reaches for the frog.
Instructor: "Say 'Yes'," and holds the frog just beyond the child's reach.
Child: "Yes."
Instructor: "Well said," and gives the child the frog for a minute.

Instructor: "Give me the frog."
Child complies.
Instructor: "That was such nice giving, you can have the frog back again," and gives the child the frog for another minute.
Instructor: "Give me the frog."
Child refuses to give the frog.
Instructor: "Give me the frog," and takes the frog from the child.
Instructor: "Do you want the frog? Say 'Yes'."
Child: "Yes."
Instructor: "OK then, let's work for it."
Instructor: "Point to the men."
Child points to the man.
Instructor: "Nice try."
Instructor: "Point to the men," and pulls the picture of the men closer to the child.
Child complies.
Instructor: "Good. Look, the frog is getting nearer," and moves the frog towards the child. (Make sure that the reinforcer—in this case, the frog—is out of the child's reach, because sometimes the child will make a grab for it.)
Instructor: "Point to the men."
Child complies.
Instructor gives the frog to the child.
When you are ready to start the teaching again, ask the child for the frog, and apply the procedure as shown above if the child refuses to give it back to you.

Here we have an excellent teaching opportunity. When the child wants something, such as the frog, you can use this reinforcer to get through as many teaching trials as you can, i.e. bringing it into the child's view, then bringing it closer to him, before finally giving him access to it. You can give the child a small amount of time with the object between items or you can say to him: "OK, you can have the frog but first you must do this and this."

You should remove the item from view if the child seems distracted by its presence. When the child answers correctly you can then bring the object into their line of vision and on the second correct trial bring it closer to him, and so on. If you are lucky and the child remains interested in the reinforcer, then stretch the teaching trials to accommodate this.

Sometimes the child sits nicely and does as asked but sometimes he will get impatient and begin to play up. To avoid this situation, try to gauge how interested he is in that particular reinforcer then set your teaching trials to accommodate this. Do not become over-zealous, and in so doing frustrate the child, as he might just close down on you or, worse, throw a tantrum.

It is important not give the child the item, just to stop him from playing up. If the worst should happen and he throws a wobbly, you'll just have to deal with it. That means completely ignoring his bad behaviour and not giving him access to the reinforcing item. When he stops making a fuss, for at least a couple of seconds, then reinforce the good behaviour (i.e. for being quiet).

If he starts making a fuss yet again, once more ignore it and wait until he goes quiet and say "Nice quiet".

If he starts making a noise again, proceed as before and wait for the chance to reinforce any good behaviour (such as "Nice sitting" or "Good quiet").

If the tantrum seems to be going on for quite a while, don't panic, it is not personal and you have all the time that it takes to wait for the child to calm down. It may seem as if this is never going to happen but hang in there because physiologically the child can not maintain this behaviour forever. In the meantime, look as though something else is occupying you, preferably something that the child will find an interest in, and the child will usually make his way over to you and become quiet while watching you.

When this eventually happens—and I have always known this to be the case—then quietly talk to the child, without any mention of his earlier behaviour.

Example

If you using picture cards during the teaching trial, then say aloud to him the things shown on the cards. Suppose at this point that the child comes and stands beside you, just continue, not giving him attention, then if he remains quiet for at least a couple of minutes say something such as "See, a clown."

If the child is paying attention and does not look as if he is going to make a fuss again, engage him further—look at him briefly and say something like: "Can you see the clown?" The child nods. Instructor: "Yes, he's got a big smiley face, see?" and points to the clown's mouth.

If the child is calm and receptive then this is sufficient. At this point you have him calm without having had to give in to him, so at this stage end the interaction such as saying: "Let's go and see what daddy is doing," and give the child your hand.

Redirect the child to something entirely different and only resume the original trial when he seems to have forgotten all about the inter-action. Preferably resume the teaching trial which led to the tantrum at a different location, so the child does not have his memory twigged by being in the same room with the same teaching unit being presented. Otherwise the same place and subject may prompt the response again. This is not to say that the item will not be eventually presented to him in that room ever again, it just means that you should lay off it for a while. Prevention is better than cure, at least it is at this stage in the campaign.

Reading and writing

To begin to teach our child to read, we shall teach him the alphabet beginning with the lower case first. We do this by means of a matching exercise, which works well for capital and small letters.

As a progression of this, we can ask our child "Which one is the small 'a'?" when presenting him with both the capital and the small letter, and so on until we are ready to match words to pictures. For this our instruction can be: "Put with same."

When the child's repertoire is expanded we shall introduce sentences for him to complete. These should include things with which he is familiar.

Example

The cat in the —-
Instructor: "What's missing?" and points to the word "hat".
Instructor: "What's missing?" and (HOH) guides the child to touch the word card "HAT".

Instructor: "That's right, HAT, see the cat in the hat," as he runs his fingers along the words in the sentence while speaking them.

The instructor can have the sentence written on a chalkboard with the missing word in - - - spaces and then (HOH) guide the child to write the missing word. Eventually he should be able to fill in the missing word unaided.

To check for understanding regarding what's been written, have some toys in front of the chalkboard and after having written the missing word the child is then instructed:

Instructor: "OK, now do it," and for our example above he puts a hat on a toy cat.
Instructor: "See, the cat in the hat."
Instructor: "Now you do it," (HOH) to help the child if necessary at this stage.

If you feel that the whole word is too much for your child to accomplish at this stage, begin with him supplying the last letter in the last word. In our previous example, "The cat in the hat" would become "The cat in the ha-". The missing letter can be at the beginning of the sentence or at the end, and on the board already in dots for the child to fill in.

In fact the sentence can be reduced to a single word and built up into a sentence. Then ask the child about the sentence e.g. "What colour is that?" If the child does not respond, tell him the answer within three seconds.

Example

Three seconds elapse.

Instructor: "The colour is red."
Instructor: "What colour is it?"
Child: "Red."
Instructor: "Red, that's right."
Instructor: "Touch red."
Child complies.
Instructor: "Good."

Instructor: "What colour is it?"
Child: "Red."
Instructor: "Well done," and gives the child a piece of chocolate.

When reading a book to your child, leave the last word for the child to read. The book should obviously be pitched at the child's level and be composed of simple sentences, which the instructor runs their finger below as the words are read aloud, which also helps the child's reading skills.

When reading to the child, ask him questions about the characters. These questions should be about the emotions of the characters, and give the child a choice of two opposite emotions such as sad or happy. Follow this by incorporating your child into the story, then ask how he might feel in that same situation.

To demonstrate this in the real world, have the child sitting ready for an ice cream, then take the ice cream away and ask: "How do you feel, happy or sad?"

The next target for our child is to re-tell the story, the aim of the exercise being for him to re-tell it in the correct order. If the child has difficulty with this, draw the sequence for him as a cue and as he progresses remove one of the pictures so he has to remember the last item, and so on until the last two pictures are removed with only the first picture acting as his guide. Obviously the aim is for all the pictures to be removed and the child to tell the story independent of any cues.

Now progress to the child making up a story. To do this, sit with him at his desk and write for him. To encourage him, say: "Let's begin, who is in our story?" This is the stage at which we begin to use those skills taught to our child earlier.

If he does not come up with any characters for the story, he will need some encouragement.

Example

Instructor: "Is our story about Teddy or Tom?"
Child: "Tom."
Instructor: "Very good."
Instructor: "What colour hair does Tom have?"
Instructor: "Where is our story happening? At the park or in the forest?"

Instructor: "Say 'The park'."

Child: "The park."

Instructor: "Fabulous."

Instructor: "What kind of day is it in our story?"

Child says nothing.

Instructor: "Is it a sunny day or a rainy day?"

If the child does not choose, then you choose for him.

Instructor: "It's a rainy day."

Instructor: "What kind of day is it?"

Child: "Rainy."

Instructor: "Yes, it's a rainy day, do we need sunglasses or Wellington boots?"

Child: "Wellington boots."

Instructor: "You remembered! Excellent."

Instructor: "So our story is about Tom at the park on a rainy day, and he is wearing his . . . ?"

Child: "Wellingtons."

Instructor: "Yes, his Wellingtons."

Instructor: "We wear our Wellingtons on a r . . ."

Child: "Rainy day."

Instructor: "That's the one."

The instructor then writes: "Tom wore his Wellington boots at the park on a rainy day."

The instructor can build up the short story by asking the child more questions.

Example

Which word is the WHO word?

What does this word say?

WHO wore the boots?

WHAT did Tom wear?

Where did Tom go?

The instructor should then ask the child to tell him about the story. In time, together they expand on the story. A useful exercise is for the instructor to ask the child to tell him some characters; these are then written on cards and put aside for another day.

Likewise, have the child give you some examples for the weather in the story (sunny, rainy, snowing, or windy) which are then made available for the child to choose from when composing their story.

As the child progresses he should be presented with choices as to how the story might begin: "Once upon a time," or "Once there was," or "A long, long time ago," and so on. This also applies to the ending. Ask him "How might our story end?" This helps him to make predictions into the future.

One problem that may occur is that the child wants the same story over and over again. To prevent this, just remove some of the components for making up the story so that he has to choose differently another time. Also, try to have him answer questions relating to who, what, when, where, why, and how.

When writing the stories, make use of prepositional phrases such as "Teddy stood behind the tree," "Cyrus stood on the step," and "Eden was in front of Tom."

The next stage is for him to understand punctuation. Use an example of a list where the word "and" is being used repetitively so that when the sentence is read back to the child he can see how this sounds and begin to learn the alternative—the art of punctuation.

The instructor can write two sentences, one a statement and the other a question, and ask the child to say which is which. For example, is it a sunny day? Then move on to the child creating a sentence referring to a picture (e.g. The boy is riding the bike).

To achieve this, begin by writing the first half of the sentence and have the second half written in dots for the child to fill in. Then do exactly the same with another sentence, only this time have three parts for him to complete (e.g. The boy is . . .). Here the child must fill in the last word without the aid of dots.

At the beginning of any task, ask: "What comes at the beginning of a sentence?" At the end of all such exercises, ask him: "What comes at the end?" so that he becomes familiar with capital letters and full stops.

If you decide to teach your child by means of the "Jolly Phonics" system, your local library should stock the book. This system gives the correct pronunciation of words, such as "o as in orange", "I as in pig", as well as the various blends such as "ea as in beauty". Teach these as any other thing that you have taught the child.

Example

Instructor: "Say 'ea'." Alternatively, write the phonic blends on the board and ask the child to underline the one that says "ea".

CHAPTER 7
Teaching seven–eight-year-olds

In this chapter we will look at perceptual motor skills for seven- and eight-year-olds.

The children in this age range have more mastery over their hands and are therefore more adept at building models and such like. For our child to achieve the same level of mastery, we need to give him as much exposure as possible to these things, such as building blocks and small model kits, nothing too painstaking or fiddly or else they are likely to give up before they have really tried.

There is nothing worse than opening a kit and finding the contents too complex to complete. So we shall begin with simple structures which we can construct beforehand and which the child needs only to finish off. This is another example of backward chaining, as we mentioned earlier when referring to completing jigsaw puzzles.

Begin with five pieces of Lego or similar (the number of pieces can be increased over time), from which we build small structures such as simple aeroplanes or houses while sitting alongside our child, who should be encouraged to watch attentively. After he has seen the finished article (in this case an aeroplane), remove the last piece and say: "Make the aeroplane." The child then completes the structure and is reinforced for this.

The next stage is for the instructor to remove two pieces from the structure and again ask: "Make the aeroplane." Continue like this until all five parts of the aeroplane have been completed.

Eventually we will be able to present our child with four or five small packets (freezer bags will do) all of which contain parts of a completed structure and all of which he has been exposed to—and is able to complete.

When the child has downtime between other programmes, these can be used as constructive fillers while the instructor prepares for the next teaching trial.

When eventually the child is proficient in making all of these structures, keep adding to them and also try to combine them in order to encourage more imaginative play. For instance, when the aeroplane is completed it can be augmented with a car and a helicopter, and a small scenario or story can be demonstrated—the aim is that the child will imitate this and add to it to carry the scene forward.

Even if he plays repetitively with these items, at least it's more constructive than twiddling the wheels, and if another child joins him he will have some basic play skills that the other child can join in with. Usually children copy other children's play far easier than they do adults.

Tying shoelaces

Although at this stage in his development our child should be able to bathe unaided, he usually still needs some assistance.

Likewise with tying shoelaces. To help the child with this tricky task, get some pieces of cardboard and make holes in them in the manner of a shoe, one for you and one for your child. Then get some thick laces—brightly coloured ones are, for obvious reasons, more interesting for the child. Then with the two of you sitting side by side, have the child copy you as you slowly feed the laces through the holes and eventually tie these together.

Reinforce every single step, then hold back on the reinforcement until finally the child can complete the task on his own, then move on to real shoes and smaller laces.

You can also buy lacing kits whereby the child can lace around the picture of a rabbit or similar. These are perhaps more interesting to children than the boring old lacing of shoes.

Fine and gross motor skills

The fine motor skills, which we practiced before, should still be practiced from time to time, as should gross motor skills. However, try to incorporate these in a natural activity so that they blend seamlessly into your child's world.

Games that are conducive to this are best given to our child when playing. Ker-Plunk, small tool kits, plastic picnic sets (where the child can spread butter using a plastic knife), and shape sorters are all good ways of embedding skills into play.

The tabletop skills we shall be concentrating on in this chapter are:

1. The manipulation of items such as safety pins, where the chills is expected to be able to pin two items together. The use of paperclips is also included in items of manipulation, as is punching holes with a hole puncher. Encourage your child to join in these activities whenever such items are in day-to-day use.
2. Cursive handwriting. Model this for the child as well as (HOH) with huge amounts of praise and great enthusiasm when showing friends and visitors your child's attempts (e.g. "Look at this, Cyrus did this all by himself. It's amazing, just like a grown-up"). The letters should be reinforced individually to begin with, eventually building these up by means of forward chaining, as we did earlier, only this time starting at the beginning rather than the end. The joy on a child's face when this skill is acquired is second to none.

We now begin to utilise those gross motor skills, beginning with the skill of jumping rope.

Rather than handing the child a set of ropes, begin with two others turning the ends of the rope with the child standing in between and jumping every time the rope is passed over his head. This is often a hit-and-miss process and is best demonstrated to the child while others perform the task. Let the child take his turn at turning one end of the rope, reinforcing him for every appropriate turn of the rope, as sometimes the child plays up by turning the rope excessively fast, for example. This is usually an avoidant tactic; having an adult (HOH) the child at the beginning is usually all that is required to make it extinct.

At this stage the child is not liable to stick at the task for long, so try to end the play session before he begins to see it as a chore. Try to stay with the theme of ropes in your play activities—there are lots of fun things you can do with him.

Examples

Twisting the rope like a tornado.
Wiggling the rope like a snake along the ground.
Using the rope as a lasso (around teddy please, rather than each other).
Tying up pirates with the rope.

All of these can be incorporated into your imaginary games together, such as snake-chasing, pirates, cowboys and Indians, and witches and goblins. Specific times of the year are obviously a good time to pull out these old familiars, then when Halloween or Christmas comes around the child has a better chance of understanding these themes and their significance.

Whenever these games are played, try to embed other skills, making sure the child is unaware of this (e.g. shooting bows and arrows for strengthening the arms and fingers). Also try ducking for apples in a bucket of water for fun, or "rowing" a cardboard box, which the child and instructor can make into an imaginary boat in one of their art sessions. The rowing motion is good for upper body strength, and to add to the fun have the instructor pull the boat across the "water" as the child rows, and if the child stops rowing the instructor stops pulling.

Likewise, the witch (the child) stirs the cauldron while saying a magic spell, this then includes voice lessons into the activity as well. The reinforcement can be that the child gets chased whenever he says the spell.

The main criterion is to think of things the child will be interested in when planning these and similar activities.

Socialisation

In this age range the child's interest in feelings begins to ignite, so now is the appropriate time to develop his abilities in this field.

For this we shall start simply with the child and instructor drawing simple faces portraying the basic emotions such as happy, sad, and angry.

Example

Instructor: "Which one is happy?" or "Which one is sad?" or "Who has got the angry face?"

This progresses to: "Show me happy," after which the child is expected to pull a happy face. Move on to ask the child questions that centre on him, based around certain scenarios (e.g. "Eden lost her doll, can you point to the picture that shows how Eden might be feeling?").

As you proceed through these teaching trials, begin to include some action cards, which can be bought from early learning centres, drawn, or cut from old catalogues. As long as there are scenes where things are happening that your child will be able to describe, the use of cards helps us to enrich his experience of the various emotions.

The cards should contain as many different outcomes as possible, and from these our child must begin to choose the correct outcome.

Example

Card number one shows a boy eating an ice cream, while card number two shows the boy dropping his ice cream.

Instructor: "How might the boy feel?"

The instructor has two cards, one with the word "Happy" written on it and another with the word "Sad". The child has to match the correct word with the correct emotion. For a verbal child, the instructor can simply ask him to say how the child might be feeling.

It may be helpful to lead the child through the scenario in his head, using a question such as: "You are waiting your turn to go on a ride at the fairground and someone pushes in front of you and takes your place. How might you feel?"

If the child still gets it wrong—and by wrong we also include any non-response—then we can give the child the correct answer.

Example

Instructor: "Someone has stolen your scooter from the playground, how do you feel?"
Child says nothing.
Instructor: "Sad."
Instructor: "How do you feel when someone steals your scooter? Sad, you would feel. Say 'Sad'."
Instructor: "How do you feel? . . . sa"
Child: "Sad."
Instructor: "That's right, you would feel SAD if someone stole your scooter."

Instructor: "When someone steals our scooter we feel, s . . ."
Child: "Sad."
Instructor: "Excellent," and gives the child a sweet.

We can begin to show our child another's perspective using the card examples. Try asking such things as: "How might the boy feel?" and "Which one do you think the boy would feel, happy or sad?"

Make the choices radically different to begin with, so that the answer is clear-cut. When the child is more able to tell the difference between the emotions, add some more emotional responses that should be more difficult to tell apart, such as: "The boy has had his scooter stolen, pick the card that tells us how the boy might be feeling." (The available choices are angry or sad. As you can see, both of these answers could be correct.)

The instructor can help the child to become clearer in his understanding of this by unexpectedly taking away his dessert just as he is about to eat it, then asking: "How do you feel?"

Of course there is always the chance that the child will remain passive and unconcerned that the dessert has been taken away from him. In this case you'll just have to give the child the answer. To expand on this programme, we can begin to ask the child questions centred on those that they might experience in their everyday life.

Everyday social skills

Now we move onto the social skills that are a necessity in everyday life, such things as: "I want to get past someone in the road, what might I say?" or "I want Eden to be my friend, what might I do?"

This part of the child's socialisation programme is ideal for introducing him into the protective issues that centre on bullying.

Examples

Johnny takes your toy, what might you do?

1. Tell Johnny to give it back.
2. Tell Johnny that you will tell a grown-up.
3. Tell your teacher.

When working in the school setting, it is usually beneficial to gauge who the group leader is in the class and befriend this child, who then befriends our child and hence we get all the others on our side too.

Receptive language

The use of language here focuses on the skill of reading. As you can see from the example above, the child is progressively being asked to use this skill more. To aid him in the process we shall introduce a matching game whereby the matching is from word to object.

This means that the child has a collection of things set before him and below these is a set of cards with the words that correspond to these objects. For instance, we might have a picture of a ball and below this a card with the word "ball" written on it.

We then give our child two word cards, one with the word "ball" and the other saying "boy", and he is expected to match the correct word to the object. Try to include a picture of the child and a word card with his name on it. Also include the family members.

Expressive language

At this stage of development a child is beginning to make inferences, and so must our child. In order to help him with this process we should introduce a variety of more complex picture cards.

So if, for example, we present our child with a picture of someone cutting the grass, we can ask: "How do we know the grass needs cutting?" If the child gets stuck, try asking him to point to the thing that's happening in the picture (in this instance, the lawnmower cutting the grass). The aim of this exercise is for the child to look for cues in the picture in order to infer what's going on—if he begins to stare at the card and lose concentration, just turn the card over.

For each card there are three elements which our child is being taught; inferential reasoning, problem solving, and determining causality.

For the teaching trial it is not necessary to have our child do all three components in one sitting, as long as these three are on your list of things to do when teaching your child about inferences.

Multiple meanings

Before dealing with these, we must build on the child's knowledge.

Example

Instructor: "How do you feel when someone gives you a present?"
Child: "Happy."
Instructor: "What's another word for happy?"
Child says nothing.
Instructor: "Pleased. Pleased is another word for happy."
Instructor: "What's another word for happy?"
Child: "Happy."
Instructor: "Pleased. Say 'Pleased'."
Child: "Pleased."
Instructor "Yes, pleased is another word for happy."
Instructor: "How might we feel if someone gives us a present, pl . . ."
Child: "Pleased."
Instructor: "Pleased. You got it right."

There are many words our child will be familiar with, and we must build on these whenever possible. So if we are talking about big and small etc, we can then apply the same method (e.g. another word for small is little, another word for big is large, and so on), all the while giving these to the child and reinforcing him as you introduce the words.

Reading

We have already addressed the basic reading skills and with these in place we can move on to the reading requirements for children of seven and eight. At this age a child is expected to be able to read a story and make connections from it to their own life, as well as being able to rephrase sentences and paragraphs.

Example

Instructor: "How else might we say this?" or "What's another word for
 . . . ?"

This builds on from our previous work. Having these programmes running back-to-back is a good idea, as the child is already familiar with what is expected of him.

The next requirement for our child is for him to be able to read a sentence and find the answer to a particular question within the sentence.

Example

Jo went to the market with her dad.
Following on from this sentence, you might ask questions such as:
"Who did Jo go to the market with?"
"Is Jo a boy or girl?"
"How did Jo and her dad get to the market?"
"What sort of things might Jo and her dad have bought at the market?"

To help the child see how information changes through out a story, it's a good idea to go back to the sequencing cards so that the child can see the sequence of events where things change.

Example

Card one has a girl with long hair.
Card two has the girl entering the hairdresser.
Card three shows the girl with her hair cut short.

Try to find examples in books, and from these we can ask the child to say how things have changed. He should be able to foresee what might happen and identify the supporting details (Instructor: "How do we know that Jo is a girl?"). The instructor can then point to the word "her" in the sentence.

The cards, which gave the child differing scenarios, can be utilised to enable our child to place these into different contexts.

Using a dictionary

Now is also the time to show our child how to use a dictionary. In this section we shall also include written directions which the child has to follow through with.

To do this you need a large writing area, a whiteboard or chalkboard, or a large sheet of paper stuck on a wall (at this stage in the child's teaching we will include an exercise that is suitable for use on a large writing area).

Something you might like to try is having the child draw a large figure eight on its side, as if they were drawing a large pair of glasses, (HOH) this at first, then let him do it on his own. This activity is supposed to be good for engaging both sides of the brain.

We can now begin to teach our child the comprehension of what he is reading. Start by writing three sentences on the board, each containing simple instructions. For our example we are going to use those that would be beneficial to our child if they were to enter the school setting.

Examples

Get your yellow folder from your book bag.
Get your pencil case from your desk.
Sit with your arms folded.

First we ask our child to read the first sentence and to underline the "important" words (HOH this if necessary). When the child has done this, say to him: "OK, now go and do it," and the child goes and acts out the sentence. When this is done we ask the child to tell us what he did.

The child then repeats what he just did, then we can move on to the next sentence. The procedure is repeated again until all of the instructions have been read and acted on. We then combine two sentences, and finally all three.

This is a good time to include time sequences, such as: "What did you do before you folded your arms?" or "What did you do after you got your yellow folder?"

When all of these requirements are in place we can then begin to introduce more to our list and continue, only this time we rub out the sentences as the child completes the tasks.

Begin by rubbing out the last sentence on the list, and so here the child is being asked to remember what was asked of him without the visual cues in place. We can help him by having him hold up three fingers and put one finger down again for each task as it is successfully completed.

In some cases children become fixated on their fingers and start staring at or twiddling them. If this should happen, just say "No", and hold their hands down for a silent count of 10, or ask him to sit on his hands or put them in his pockets. Reinforce this behaviour before continuing, only this time the instructor holds up their fingers for the count. (Try to eliminate the finger cues as soon as possible.)

Now we are beginning to generalise some of our other programmes, in this case the "before and after" programme, while simultaneously helping our child with his recall skills.

Writing

Writing entails so much more when the child reaches this age group, as the skills that he is expected to grasp are much more complex at this stage of development. Tasks might include doing research for a report, sketching the plot of a story, writing a topic sentence that has a main idea, writing a description in a paragraph, running two sentences together, writing a dialogue that contains adjectives and adverbs, writing about cause and effect, and supporting a main idea using details. This might seem a lot, but it is what would be expected of a typically developing child.

These tasks might take our child longer but of course he has a helper who uses positive reinforcement to enable the child to move forward at a quicker pace—but remember to move only at the pace of the child, not the material.

We shall now systematically weave our way through these requirements, working at the pace of the child. So what if our child never writes a report, he didn't want to be a pen-pusher anyway . . .

The first item on our list is researching a report. This is best done around a local issue, one that the child can feel a part of, things that are perhaps in the media's eye such as the removal of red post boxes in London, or a new arrival at the local zoo, or the World Cup.

Our instructors task, in this case, is to scan the news coverage with the child, who then cuts out the newspaper articles about his chosen topic before the instructor and child go off and do something around these themes (e.g. post a letter, visit the zoo). These can then be pasted and stuck into an exercise book, again we are utilising those skills that our child has already learned.

Finally the child and instructor can compose a sentence together about one of the pictures. The child can stick this into his exercise book and write a sentence underneath to explain it.

Here we have a naturally occurring moment in which to practice prepositions ("We are going to write a sentence under our picture, where is under the picture?").

Example

Instructor: "Point to under."
Child does nothing.
Instructor: "Point to under," and (HOH) guides the child to point to under the picture.
Instructor: "Marvellous."
Instructor: "Where do we write our sentence?"
Child points to under the picture.
Instructor: "You are absolutely right."
Instructor: "Where is this?" and points to under the picture.
Child: "Under."
Instructor: "Well done! Congratulations, your sweet is under your chair."

The next item on our list is to construct the plot of a story. The instructor begins by writing a title for the story, such as "Cyrus went to the park".

At this stage the instructor should give the child a felt tip pen and ask him to underline the WHO word in the sentence—this may need explaining. To check whether the child has understood this information, ask him to tell you another WHO word.

For the second stage, the instructor gives the child another felt tip pen—a different colour—and this time asks the child to underline the DOING word. Again, this may need explaining, just do as you did for the example above.

The third stage is for the child to underline the WHERE word in a different colour.

The instructor can help by asking the child to go through the events in the story ("And then what happens?"). If the child gets stuck, all the instructor has to do is give him some examples to choose from.

The process is similarl with topic sentences—again the instructor can give the child an example and point out the main idea to him.

Example

Topic sentence: Animals that live in the jungle.

To write a descriptive phrase and clause our instructor can draw on the material from the section where our child was required to "Tell us something about . . ." only this time the child is being asked to write, rather than say, what happened. It might be helpful to give the child a picture of the objects or people whom they are being asked to write about, and first have him do the task orally before asking him to write.

Using the example of three pictures of children, two boys and one girl, we then ask the child to describe what he sees (e.g., the boys have got short hair and the girl has long hair, the boys are wearing glasses). He will more than likely need help with this exercise—to do so, the instructor should sit with the child and have the three pictures in front of him, and then proceed to lead the child through the pictures, asking him to give you the picture that does not have a boy in it, or the picture were the boy is jumping etc.

Gender awareness can be raised by including a "sort" programme, in which the instructor asks the child to "sort" all the boys from the girls in a pile of pictures. Then, "Give me all the boys," or "Give me all the girls."

For the combination of two simple sentences we shall concentrate on gender, and so here we have a single card with the word "boy" on it. Under this card we place two other cards with the words "he" and "she" on them and then we ask our child to match the word to the card.

We can then introduce "it" to the equation by asking such things as: "Is a tree a girl?" or "Is a cat a boy or an it?"

This is a classifying pronouns programme, where our child is being asked another word for "boy" (answers: he, him, his, man). Alternatives to "girl" include; her, she, hers, lady. After this has been done, return to the task of writing the sentence combinations (the boy is riding his bike, the girl is eating her ice cream).

A fun way to teach dialogue is for the child to write something and then the instructor writes something in reply. The child writes a reply to this, and so on. (Using different coloured pens is useful for this exercise.)

Yet another skill that will be required of our child is that he can use adjectives and adverbs when describing things. For writing our story, we should give our child some choice cards containing elements that might appear in the story (is it a sunny day, a rainy day, or a windy day, and so on). Produce a selection of hand-drawn cards with pictures of the sun, a cloud, raindrops, or an umbrella blown inside-out to denote these weather features.

We give these to our child, along with another set of word cards which correspond to the picture cards, and again we ask him to match the word cards to the picture cards. When this is done the child can pick out one of the weather cards to use in his story.

When the story is written, we take the child back over it and ask him to underline all the "describing" words, "doing" words, "who" words etc, until eventually he can remember that all the "who" words are underlined in orange and all the "doing" words are underlined in green, for instance.

Make sure he becomes familiar with writing cause and effect in his stories, as well as having him fill in the details that support the main idea.

Examples

Why did they put up their umbrellas?
Why do we wash our hands before we eat?
Why is Sara crying?

We shall now enhance the skills already encountered for these age groups, utilising the fine motor skills that we painstakingly established for our child as we endeavour to create situations where our child can make use of them.

The child is now at the stage where modesty is being aroused and he is usually starting to close the bathroom door when taking a bath (which he should be doing independently by now).

Children in this age group are well able to manipulate a knife while eating and should also be able to peel an apple with the knife—practice is the order of the day here.

To ensure that our child is using the full extent of his language, try such things as setting a bowl of soup in front of him without giving him a spoon. Then we can ask: "What do you want?" Remember to only accept the correct response, no letting the child guide your hand, or giving in to him to make your life easier.

Here are some skills that can be discretely introduced to the child in the natural environment. As the family sits down to lunch, the people seated near the child can subtly reinforce him by saying: "Hey everyone, look at Jamie, he is so good at peeling his apple." Or at picnics, allow him to help with the preparations, such as spreading butter on bread and cutting sandwiches.

At this age a child is able to beat an egg in a bowl without spillage, so we should encourage our child to participate in baking, as this is useful for teaching this skill implicitly in the natural setting. Other tasks the child and instructor can do together to enhance manual dexterity are making paper hats and paper aeroplanes. (Sticking small pieces of sticky tape on the child's fingers is helpful in making him aware of individual fingers. You can then draw faces on the child's fingers and have a finger puppet shows, which further enhance his fine motor skills.)

For the gross motor skill, the skip, girls seem to outshine boys in this age bracket. For teaching this skill, it may be best to have another child model this for our child, who can be helped along by the instructor who can break down the activity into small steps, then reinforcement is built up as in a chaining. It is usually helpful for the instructor to make a small list of all the necessary stages for such skills.

Example

Skipping rope: Child holding the rope in the ready position to pull over his head.
Child turns the rope over his head.
Child jumps over the rope as it comes over his head.
Child repeats this action twice.

Try having the instructor with the child in front of him and the two skipping together—the instructor must tell the child when to jump, and reinforce him as they do so. Build up your chain according to your list.

The skills to work towards are for the child to be able to safely operate tools such as a hammer, a screwdriver, and pliers.

Socialisation

As our child begins to mature his self-awareness becomes more noticeable. At this stage of development children usually prefer to mix with the same gender—this is something to be aware of when initiating play dates.

When endeavouring to teach other skills the use of peers is preferable, as at this age the child is more prone to peer pressure, and will tend to copy someone his own age rather than an adult. Peers are a valuable commodity when teaching children, as they are a means of monitoring skills, and are supreme for supplying examples for any consequences of behaviour.

Theory of mind test

Typically, developing children are said to be able to think about thinking, something that is important for learning and cognitive development.

The Theory of Mind Tests are used as an indicator towards comprehending whether your child has an understanding of other minds and, as such, are a way of understanding the inferential process. Children are given the theory of mind test, which studies "out of date beliefs", at about four years of age.

In test one (see below), four-year-old children were able to successfully complete the test, whereas of the children who have the diagnosis of autism, only 23 per cent got the test right.

Test two is an example of a child's understanding of an "out of date" photograph. 100 per cent of the children on the autistic spectrum got this test right, with only 70 per cent of the "ordinary" four-year-olds getting it right.

You may wish to try these tests for yourselves, examples of which are set out below.

Stephanie Louise

Test one

Have the instructor, child, and another person sit in a room with two containers. With the other two looking on, the instructor puts a marble into one of the containers and then leaves the room. Then, with the child looking on, the other person in the room with the child removes the marble from the box, where the instructor had put it, and places it in the other box. The child is then asked: "Where do you think the instructor will look for the marble?"

If correct, the child will say that the instructor will look for the marble where he put it before leaving the room. If incorrect, the child will assume that the instructor will look for the marble where the person put it after the instructor had left the room.

Test two

The instructor, with the child looking on, takes a picture of a toy cat sitting in a chair. The instructor then puts the picture of the cat on a bed, and then asks the child: "In the picture, where is the cat?"

What we are looking for here is whether our child has the ability to work backwards in his mind.

CHAPTER 8
Play skills

Play

Here the focus is on play skills—although there have been many references to play thus far, now is the time to take a more detailed look at how to implement various skills.

We begin this process with our initial introduction to the child. This section is obviously aimed at the instructors, who might not necessarily be the parents, however the play as presented here is for all those endeavouring to teach a child on the autistic spectrum.

How to conduct that first encounter

To begin with the child will usually try to avoid eye contact, but remain alert and watch for that sneaky glance towards you—these children are, like all other human beings, curious creatures, and be in no doubt that they will be scrutinising you in their own way. It is your job to capture this moment; wink, smile, wave, do as you will, but make that first contact positive.

The next step is to get down to the child's eye level and introduce yourself. Asking for eye contact at this stage is not something I'd advise, because you are seeking a friend here—if the child thinks you are just another person trying to influence him, your chances of really getting him on your side are slim. Always speak *to* him, not *at* him.

Assuming that all is going well and the child is warming to you, let's move to the next stage, the actual engaging in interactive play.

How?

The first thing to do is to acquire some insight into what sort of things the child likes doing or eating. As an example, let's assume that he likes raisins and his Gameboy.

Begin by approaching the child as he plays with his game, not too close at first, watching as though he were a stranger on a train and you're trying to look in on his game. In time move closer and give some positive feedback relating to the game ("Hey, that was a great move you just made,")—appear engrossed in the game, not the child.

As time moves on, start eating some raisins and give a few to the child, all the while acting as though you're totally absorbed in the game.

That's more than enough for a first encounter. When it's time to leave, don't insist on the child saying goodbye, but make sure you say goodbye, then say something positive about the child to his mother (carer) within earshot of the child—you can be sure he'll be listening.

On the next encounter bring something fun and reinforcing with you, an item that will cause him to look away from his Gameboy and focus on the toy you have brought. There is always something that will catch his attention, particularly a toy that lights up and makes a noise.

Hopefully the new toy has worked and you have received that first glance from the child, signalling his interest. Now go and play with this object beside the child. If you're fortunate enough and the child comes to you you're already over the first hurdle. The child wants your item, yet he can only have it on your terms—try not to make this too obvious.

Example

Instructor: "You want this?"
Child reaches for the item.
The instructor gently blocks his access to the toy.
Instructor: "Say 'Yes'."
Child: "Yes."
Instructor: "Well said," and gives the child the item.

This is how your second encounter with the child should resolve itself.

For your next meeting, think of some other thing that the child might like and proceed as before, only this time request more interaction from him.

So as the child again approaches you for your toy, this time ask him to give you his toy in return for you giving him yours, reinforce this and carry on. Let the play unfold naturally from then on. You've made a friend, now cultivate that friendship, always letting him take the lead and always subtly reinforcing, whether verbally or with tangibles. The trick is to make the interaction seem natural, not an unequal relationship such as that between a pupil and teacher.

As time unfolds the child will seek you out to have fun with, and that is the moment at which we can begin to teach different play skills.

Example

Instructor: "OK little fellow, so you want to play wizards and dragons today, do you? Well that's OK, but who is going to be the dragon?"

It's usually you, but the child takes delight in assigning this role to you. Let him do so BUT only on condition that first you both do this boring stuff, i.e. 15 minutes of teaching time at the table. Start to prolong this teaching time at every opportunity, as this enables the child to extend his attention span and his waiting skills.

When engaged in the play, insist at the right moment (when the child is fully engrossed in the game), that it's your turn to be the wizard. Ask the child such things as: "What does the wizard look like? And what does a wizard do?" This acting on your part must be convincing, so brush up on your acting skills!

So you see how the child is gradually lured into the interaction as a willing partner.

At this stage, it's a good idea to introduce a "real and pretend" programme, which should proceed something like this:

Example

The instructor sits at the table with the child. On the table there is a real piece of fruit and a plastic piece of fruit.

Instructor: "Is this real?" and picks up the plastic piece of fruit and tries to bite it.
Instructor: "Just pretending."
Instructor: "Is this real or pretend?"
Child says nothing.
Instructor: "It's real. Say 'Real'."
Child: "Real."
Instructor: "Excellent, it is real."
Instructor: "So this one must be pre . . . ," and points to the other item.
Child says nothing.
Instructor: "Touch the real one."
Child does nothing.
Instructor: "Touch the real one," and (HOH) guides the child's hand to touch the real one. "Good."

113

Instructor: "Touch the real one."
Child touches the real one.
Instructor: "That's the one."
Instructor: "Which one is real?"
Child does nothing.
Instructor: "Which one is real?" and points to the real one.
Instructor: "Where is the real one?"
Child touches the real one.
Instructor: "You were amazing! Go and play."
The child goes to play but wants the instructor to play with him.
Instructor: "Hey little one, looks like you want to play our game again?"
Child: "Yes."
Instructor: "OK then."
Instructor: "First, let's quickly do this [the teaching task] and then we can play our game. Can I be the dragon?"
Child: "Yes".
Instructor: "Well OK then, let's get this done and I'll be the dragon. And so who will you be?"
Child: "The wizard."
Instructor: "Oh no! Not the wizard! I wonder what a wizard might do? Does he cast spells?"
Child: "Yes."
Instructor: "Oh no! Not a spell."
Instructor: "Can you turn me into a frog with your spell, Mister wizard?"
Chil: "Yes."
Instructor: "And you want to play that game?"
Child nods his head.
Instructor: "Is that a yes?" (Always remember to try and pull that language out of him at every opportunity!)
Child: "Yes."
Instructor: "Well, come on then, let's get this done first," and motions towards the table where the work is already set out for him to do. Both of you sit down at the table and begin to do the real/pretend unit once again.

In this way the teaching trial begins once again, with the child as a willing subject.

Obviously the real and pretend items must vary, so think of as many things as you can to introduce to the child. Try to vary the way you

114

ask for the items at each trial, so rather than saying "Where is the pretend one," or "Touch the real one," ask the child for some language such as: "So if this one is pretend, then that one must be re . . . ?" or "What's that one?" and point to the pretend one.

Make the child aware of your use of language, using "This" and "That" when referring to the items. During play, say something to the effect of: "Hey, would that be real or pretend?"

Outdoor play

You decide to take the child to the park to play on the swings, only to discover that he is fearful of the swing.

First show him what fun you are having while swinging up as high as you can on the swing. Please ensure that the child is not standing too close, and that you can bring the swing down in time to avoid a collision!

What do you do if the child is stuck on the roundabout watching you from a distance, or seems to be completely ignoring you?

First make sure that your relationship with the child is sound, for this procedure is rather intrusive and will only be tolerated from someone he trusts.

This being so, then call the child over to where you are, preferably when he is beginning to get thirsty or a bit peckish. Let him have a drink or a nibble just for coming towards the dreaded object (the swing).

On another occasion do exactly the same, only this time say to the child: "You can have it, BUT first you must swing for a little while with me."

The reason we're not yet asking the child to swing independently is that you have the power to make your swing reinforcing—the chances of him sitting on a swing by himself and finding this reinforcing are, at this stage, remote.

So as soon as the child climbs on your knee, give him a nibble or the carton of juice to hold, and work up on the swing until the child is unable to get off. Keep swinging, even if he drops the juice—and they usually do—while clinging to you for dear life.

Stay up there until the resistance has subsided, then say: "OK? You see, that wasn't so bad, was it?" The chances are that he will want to repeat the activity, but remember that the goal is to eventually get him swinging on his own swing.

So there you both are, the child glancing in your direction from time to time as you swing on the swing. This time he is clued up as to what's happening, so the chances of him coming over to get anything such as a drink from you is slight. So when the child is off guard, grab him and put him on your knee, and swing with him yet again.

He will kick and protest, but just keep going, stay on the swing and say nothing until the protest has subsided and go on swinging for at least half an hour. During that time, sing, point things out to him (the sky, birds in the trees, dogs on the ground) and make it fun: "Hey, look at us, almost to the sky."

This usually solves the problem of reluctance. If it doesn't, then the next time the child wants anything really badly make it on condition that they go on the swing with you for a little while.

When the time comes that the child actively enjoys this, then this swinging on your knee becomes "only" on condition that he sits on his own swing by himself. If he gets up from his swing too soon and wants to get on your swing with you, then say: "That was too quick, you have to sit longer on your own swing." A couple of minutes should suffice.

The problem of him wanting to swing only while sitting on your knee—refusing to sit on his own swing—is overcome by first asking him to sit on his own swing and swing for a bit, after which he can then come and sit with you.

A time will come when the child goes along with this—at this stage jump off and, while holding him on the swing, make his swing go higher in the air. Reinforce this, ignoring any protests, and then when you think it's safe to do so, let him go, and highly reinforce this.

What if he falls off? In my experience, it is extremely unlikely because the law of self-preservation usually kicks in, and the child usually feels rather impressed with himself.

This is what childhood is all about, trial and error. Don't deny the child a chance to experience this because YOU are too afraid—we are not talking about the child swinging precariously high in the sky, screaming, while you look on. All we are doing is guiding him over the threshold of fear.

This is where it pays to have an experienced instructor, someone who knows children and preferably someone with experience of childrearing. This is because you usually find that the parents pussyfoot around the child, afraid that they might break him. There is nothing wrong with this, because—rightly—their child is precious, but it is counter productive when it holds the child back.

Indoor play

Earlier, we taught examples of play such as jigsaws, model building, and ball skills, by means of backward chaining. These are now our basic building blocks, from which we shall encourage our child to play independently. Items of play should be age-appropriate.

Many a child on the autistic spectrum will play obsessively with the same thing. To discourage this, we shall begin to teach our child "transitional skills".

To do this, we begin with three play activities spread out in front of the child—these should be from the items the child has already been exposed to in earlier teaching trials.

Begin working from right to left with the child going over each item, each of which has been almost completed (backward chained). For instance, use a jigsaw puzzle which is complete except for two pieces (extend this over time, with the aim of him having to complete the whole puzzle from scratch).

Activity number two can consist of a small pile of building blocks that have been built up as a tower with some remaining blocks beside it, which the child adds to the structure. The third activity can be a toy car.

Example

Instructor: "Let's play," and guides the child, from left to right, to the first item. If he is reluctant, (HOH) guide him to complete the puzzle. When this is achieved, the instructor praises the child and guides him (points) to the second item, without any language. When this is complete, the instructor again reinforces the child, who is then guided to the third item—remember that pushing, not pulling, is the appropriate use of a toy car. Only when he has learned to play with the item appropriately is he allowed to vary the way in which he uses it.

You may find that the child wants to strike at the building blocks rather than adding more to the top of an existing structure. No matter how much fun it might be to demonstrate how to make the blocks come tumbling down, it is perhaps best to refrain from this when initially teaching him the building skills.

If the child is more interested in demolition than destruction, first give him a verbal warning. If he persists, tell him that he will be permitted to swipe away the blocks ONLY after he has finished building the structure. If he is determined to swipe after you have told him this, then the thing to do is to put a punisher on it (when you do something aversive rather than reinforcing).

Using the punisher

In the case of swiping the blocks, have a bucket of additional blocks, a packet of pasta shapes or cotton wool balls to hand. When the child swipes, you empty these on the floor and tell the child to pick them up—one at a time. If the child protests then (HOH) assist him in the picking up process, but only at the beginning as he is expected to complete this task unaided. If he picks up more than one item at a time, stop him from doing this (HOH) and remember not to engage him with language or eye contact.

When the picking-up task is complete, the child is non-verbally guided back to the original block-building activity, which he must complete. Should he decide to swipe again, apply the same procedure only this time, rather than going back to the building activity, take him right back to the beginning of the play items.

The correction procedure should be applied whenever the child uses an activity inappropriately.

When the sequence of play is complete, highly reinforce the child for this and release him from the learning environment.

As time goes on change the items being presented to the child, keeping only one of the initial items, which you can use as the first item in a new sequence.

Television, video and DVD

The play modules would not be complete without a section on these. When our child wishes to watch films, we must insist that he watches the screen in an appropriate manner (sitting nicely and not twiddling with the apparatus). If you encounter any problems in this area, this section will show you how to combat any issues that may arise.

First, the choice of film must be rotated, to prevent the child from obsessing on any particular film. To do this, simply tell him that he can have his choice of film "only" if the instructor/mum/dad get to watch their choice on the following occasion. If the child throws a wobbly when you try to watch something other than his choice, just ignore this behaviour and proceed to watch your choice.

Pretend to be enthralled by your choice of film and wait for the child to settle down. A few minutes after he has stopped making a fuss, turn off the machine and engage the child in something away from the TV.

When the child gets to watch another film he must remain seated. If he gets up from his seat, warn him that the TV will be switched off if he doesn't sit nicely and watch. If he gets up from his seat a second time, switch off the TV and go to some other, lesser-preferred activity, (HOH) that activity if necessary.

When the child is quiet, reinforce this behaviour, or indeed any good behaviour, to distract him from the maladaptive behaviour that he has been exhibiting.

After the child seems to have forgotten the incident, usually 10 or 20 minutes later, return to the original point of contention and try again. Tell the child what is expected of him ("We are going to watch your choice of DVD now, and tomorrow we shall watch my choice. You have to sit nicely and not twiddle with the machine, is that OK?") Have the child agree—if at any stage he breaks the agreement, remind him of it. This usually settles him down, but if he insists on rewinding the video or getting up and down from his seat, switch off the machine without entering into any debate with him. Then, the following day, as promised, settle down with the child and begin to watch your choice of film. As soon as the child starts to misbehave, switch off the machine, and leave the TV room.

As time passes, and the child has refrained from rewinding the machine and is settled down nicely watching the film, walk out of the room and take the remote control with you. If the child attempts to get up and walk around or tries to rewind the film in your absence, then switch off the machine from where you are, out of sight of the child. Likewise, if you are sitting with the child and he gets up from his seat, remind him of your agreement—if he still gets up from his seat, apply the above procedure again. (Try to have 20-minute breaks between trials.)

When the child is sitting nicely and watching appropriately, reinforce this good behaviour by giving him small pieces of a reinforcer, things that are usually associated with watching film such as popcorn or jellybeans.

Play dates

First, decide on the activities you shall engage the children in beforehand—knowing what the other child likes to play and eat will help greatly with this.

Arrange the play date at a time when the children are still alert and willing to engage (preferably not when they are tired after a day at school). If, however, this is the only available time, then have the play date centre on less physical activities such as watching films or doing art projects.

Keep the play dates short to begin with, and end them with a small snack for the children, and a tangible reinforcer for the visiting child to take away.

Before your child's guest arrives, cue your child as to what he should say when they reach the door. When the doorbell rings, cue the child to say: "Hello Sam. Come and see my toys." When the play date is over, cue the child to say: "Thank you for coming to play." While the play date is in full swing, reinforce the children for being in close proximity: "You two are playing so nicely together."

Try to make sure that the other child is enjoying his visit so that he will want to come back again. As mentioned above, set the activities to the visiting child's preferences—if he is good at board games, centre the play date mainly on this topic, and practice this type of game beforehand with your child so that he will be ready for this.

120

Make a note of all the games that the children enjoyed and those they didn't, so that on another occasion you won't be wasting time trying to engage them in activities which they find uninteresting.

The instructor should phase himself or herself out of the interaction as soon as possible, watching the children discretely from a distance. If their attention seems to waning, go in and engage them in some activity where three or more players are required. The initial interaction may only be productive for the first 15 minutes—don't try to prolong it at this stage, just go with the flow.

Try both indoor and outdoor activities, making them as enjoyable as possible, and always reinforce the children for playing nicely together.

CHAPTER 9

The development of emotional health

This chapter looks at the development of emotional health and provides examples of different strategies that you might find helpful.

The emotional parts of the teaching, as have already been applied elsewhere in this book, will act as a cornerstone for you to work from. Examples include the "what's happening?" questions, "how might you feel if?" questions, and using drawing skills to communicate emotional states. The examples given are set out as a guide to help you see how these techniques have be applied.

This chapter, as for the previous chapter on play, is best suited to the independent agent (the instructor). If, however, this is not possible, then use this material as best you can and apply it wherever possible.

The first thing we shall do is to erect a safe environment for our child. Begin by setting some ground rules—our child will already be familiar with some rules, as he was introduced to them in the groupwork sessions. Start with a large piece of paper (the back of an old roll of wallpaper will do) on which you write, in large characters, the rules that you "both" come up with. The rules should centre on your own and the child's safety.

Emotions

Examples

We stay in the room.
No throwing or breaking things.
No hitting each other.

At this point the instructor should inform the child that whatever is said in the room, stays in the room ("I [the instructor] will not tell anybody else what you tell me, except if what you tell me means that you may be hurt in some way, like if you stop taking your medicine or if someone is hurting or being unkind to you."). Also, inform the child that you will always inform him beforehand if you intend to tell someone else, and that the child will then be given the chance to tell the other person himself, if he so chooses.

The child may well confide in the instructor, and tell him of something that happened to him a long time ago. If this should be the case, please refrain from saying "Why didn't you tell someone?", as this can only add to the child's sense of guilt and maight make him feel even worse about the incident.

Let the child know that if, at any time, any of the rules are broken the session will be stopped, but that he is welcome to come back again for another session.

After this has been agreed, both of you should make a mark on the paper, to show that you both agree. This can be a handprint or writing your names, or applying stickers to the paper.

Establishing trust

The session should be held in private, where there will be no interruptions and where the environment is safe and where there is room for the instructor and child to move around freely.

The session should run for an hour—time boundaries should be set and adhered to. The instructor must keep an eye on the time and tell the child when the time is about up. If the child insists on bringing important issues to the fore as the session is about to conclude, the instructor should tell the child that they will speak about this at his next session. The child must not be allowed to take control of the session, such as by moving the times around or going over time. This acts as a secure base from which the child can feel contained.

The rules that the instructor and child have established should be written down and displayed whenever the session is running.

Session one

The instructor and child sit together in the room and each has a large sheet of paper in front of him and some felt tip pens. This session should be conducted in silence—if the child makes to leave the room, you need to remind him of the rules.

The instructor should then begin to draw on his piece of paper. Whatever the child does, the instructor should imitate (any speech, flapping his hands) and if the child begins to shout try lowering your voice, as this sometimes helps to bring his volume down.

At the end of the session thank the child for coming and tell him that you look forward to your next meeting.

Session two

The child arrives and the rules are on display. The paper and pens are set out as before, but this time the instructor speaks to the child.

Example

Instructor: "Draw Cyrus."
The child draws a head with eyes, nose, and mouth.
Instructor: "Good."
Instructor: "What's happening in the picture?"
Child: "Cyrus crying," and draws tears falling from the eyes of the child in the picture.

At this point in the interaction the instructor should give the child access to other art materials such as a paint set, glue, and glitter, and allow the child to do as he pleases for the duration of the interaction.

If the child gets up from the table and goes elsewhere then the instructor should follow, without mentioning anything that has gone on before, unless the child does so. The place where the child has moved to should have different toys, such as small figures, dressing up clothes, and books. The instructor again follows the child's lead.

At the end of the session do not clear away the original materials, instead ask the child: "What shall we do with these?" If the child remains silent say: "You can take them with you, would you like that?" or "Shall we tidy them away?" or "Maybe we can throw them away?" Then act as the moment dictates.

If the child protests at these items being touched, then remember where everything is. To help with this, compose a quick mental map and, when the child goes, draw an actual map so that you can remember replicate the layout for your next meeting.

Session three

When the child returns, everything is set out as before. The best rule for instructors to apply is to remain silent as much as possible. We humans like to fill silence, but it should be filled by the child, not the instructor. This may not always be through speech, it could be through painting, drawing, and the other materials in the room.

At this stage the instructor should draw a picture of himself and say: "I'm drawing a picture of me," and draw a picture including his head, facial components, body, and limbs, all the while naming the components as they are drawn. Now the child knows how to draw a full person—this is one of the developmental landmarks of a child of five years.

Don't worry if the child repeatedly keeps drawing only a head—this is where they need to be at that moment in time, for whatever reason. Here, the instructor can perhaps help the child to move forward by asking such things as: "Where is the body?"

If the child moves away from the table, you might find the "stuck in the mud" game useful. Here the child and instructor pretend to pull the child's feet free from imaginary mud. Then, after a couple of minutes, the game switches to floating on the moon, where the two mimic a sense of weightlessness (signifying freedom, the opposite of being stuck in the mud). The game switches back and forth between the two states.

Questions that may help while the child is doing the activity are: "I wonder what might happen next?" or "I wonder when Cyrus will be happy again?"

If the child draws another person, ask: "Who is it?" "What is happening?" "What is X feeling/doing?" If the child draws a number of people, ask him to say who they are—if they are family members, keep an eye out for one of them being omitted from the drawing, or perhaps the child leaves himself out of the equation.

The instructor can then help the child open up some more by saying: "I wonder what's going on?" or "Where is Cyrus?"

When our child begins to draw a figure with more than a head, we could perhaps view this as a success, as he has obviously moved forward in terms of developmental landmarks.

Now we will concentrate on those moments away from the table where there are books and small figures, as mentioned earlier. The figures are a way for the child to enact his story, for instance he may throw them away or hide one figure while still playing with the others. There is no need for interpretation; at this stage all that is required is for the instructor to listen to the child.

Do not tidy away the figures at the end of the session or say something to the effect of: "Let's bring that little figure back, it looks lonely over there." It's better to say things like: "That little figure looks like it is hiding, I wonder if he'll come out from hiding?"

If the child has been on holiday, the instructor can ask him to draw where he went, what he did, and how he felt.

If the child scribbles angrily, say words to the effect of: "That looks like an angry scribble."

If the child insists on always colouring in black, say: "That looks like a sad colour." If he says "Yes," you then ask: "Will there come a time when the colour won't be sad?" When the child eventually chooses another colour we can perhaps assume that he is moving through his emotions.

Although interpretation is not necessary, I have found it useful to apply a mode of experience, as set out below, when working with a child in this capacity. These assumptions are intended as a guide and are not set in stone, so use them as you wish. Equally, discard them if you need to.

Strategies

Examples

When the child insists on using black, this may well be his way of conveying sadness or depression. It has been said that depression is a wall against anger, and if this is so you may well find that as the black drawings give way, the child may actually begin to express his underlying sadness (such as by crying).

The black drawings may give way to red drawings, red being the colour of anger. What we then experience are more expressions of anger in our child's behaviour, so we must try and encourage him to express his anger in a more appropriate way, such as through art or play, even hitting a cushion with a tennis racket. In this latter instance, the instructor can model this behaviour for the child, who may or may not choose to follow suit. What you usually find is that as the anger subsides, the emotion of anger gives way to sorrow.

If the child insists on aggressively banging the little figures together try stating: "They seem angry." Or we can intervene, and use a superhero figure to show the child that new ways of dealing with a situation are possible.

Over time, the child should begin to play with the toys in a different manner, and may begin to use more colourful pens. He may even begin to draw rainbows and happy people in his pictures. If this happens, I would suggest that perhaps the child has resolved something, although we will never truly know if this is the case. What we can be certain of is that the child has a happier disposition as displayed through his behaviour and we can see from his artwork that he has reached developmental landmarks that were not present to begin with (the example above of drawing a full-bodied figure rather than just a head).

As the child moves through his emotional states (crying, anger, aloofness etc), always remind yourself that these emotions are not directed at you personally, that his expressions of pent-up emotions are nothing to do with you.

Also try to be aware of your need to rush in and make things better for the child—this is a natural tendency, and one that you'll no doubt encounter many times in the course of your work. You may fall down on this one many times before you master it but, rest assured, all that is required of you, as a normal human being, is that you get back in the race again. Try, try and try again.

To stand back and watch the suffering of another is very difficult, especially where a child is concerned, but it's something you must do in this instance. Rushing in and rescuing the child is to do him a disservice—remember, we are attempting to install in him skills that will serve him all his life, when we the parents or instructors are no longer there for him.

Learning to deal with one's own emotions is a monumental task and it is something that you and the child will be learning to do together. At such times it maybe helpful to remind yourself of the fact that some things can't be made better—as much as we'd like to, we can't bring back a lost sibling or parent. In such cases, all that we, as caring adults, can do is to help our child to express his emotions in a safe environment.

Case studies

In this section we shall look at some scenarios in which behaviourism meets psychotherapy.

Example one

Here we have a little girl who keeps taking the heads off her dolls and throwing them away, then wanting to go and fetch them.

What's going on? What can the instructor do to help her?

The instructor ran the sessions as set out above, and as the child began to open up she revealed: "Mummy says I'm clever."

Having spoken to the mother, it was obvious that she was proud of her child's intelligence, but it was also revealed that she had wanted a male child.

The mother always encouraged the child in her academic endeavours: when they were out walking, the child was told all the answers before the questions were posed. An example of this was when they spotted a bird and the mother began telling the child all the various classification of the bird—in effect the child was not being allowed to take simple pleasure in seeing a bird, rather she would begin frantically searching for the categorisation of the bird and in so doing please mummy. As such she was living up to mummy's expectations of her; to be clever.

The instructor in this case was able to inform the mother of this and she was made aware of how she may have been contributing to this behaviour in her daughter.

When in a session the child was told by the instructor that, yes, she was clever, but she was also kind, and funny, and thoughtful, and so on—that she was more than just a head, a brain, and a clever person—the result was that the child stopped removing her dolls' heads and the mother stopped trying to help her be clever.

Mother and child then settled into a more harmonious relationship, and the child was integrated into mainstream school—her maladaptive behaviour had precluded this before.

Example two

A child was being very disruptive in the classroom setting. The instructors could not take him from the classroom while this was happening—to do so would be to reinforce the disruptive behaviour (the child's' reasoning being, "If I make a fuss then I'll be taken away from the situation that I'm protesting against").

In this case a calming strategy was applied. The instructor applied deep pressure to the child's hands by pushing and pulling his finger joints one at a time, beginning with the middle finger, until he calmed down. (Instructors should try this calming strategy beforehand to see how long it takes for the effect to occur and for how long, as children's responses to this technique vary. When the effect has set in, this will give the instructor long enough to take the child outside, without reinforcing the maladaptive behaviour, hence the reinforcement follows on from the desired behaviour, calmness.)

When the child was taken outside he was allowed to run off his energy, and then a calming strategy was again applied—the child was taken on the instructor's knee on the swing, and the two swung to and fro, thus calming the child (this activity was known to be something that the child liked).

When the instructor was ready to leave this activity she informed the child that, in five minutes, they would return home. However, the child then threw a big tantrum, and so at this point the instructor applied a behavioural strategy (extinction) to take control of the situation, not allowing the child to take control. So then without language, or eye contact, the child was taken home. If he refused to walk, he was carried.

By the time the child reached home he was already in a calmer state, as physiologically a child cannot sustain this heightened state of arousal beyond a certain threshold—what happens is that a feedback system kicks in and the body returns to a calmer state naturally.

When at home the child was given a sheet of paper and then told that he could draw how he was feeling. After he had done this he was then taken back out to the swings. In this instance the child was not told beforehand that if he completed the task then he could return to the swings in the park, as in this particular case the child often resorted to oppositional behaviour.

Whatever the instructor said was adhered to. If, when asked if he wanted go to the swings, the child then said no, that was that and he was not allowed to change his mind. The instructor had informed the child at the outset that whatever the child said first was what they would stick to. If the child protested, this was worked through as above, and the child was not allowed to change his mind.

When, at home, the child was doing the original activity which had led to his protests in the school situation (in this case his reading), the instructor began by sitting down with him with a picture of his classroom set out before him, together with his pencil case and other items familiar to the school setting. The same reading book was used and the situation was worked through again, and the child was only taken back to the swings when he had calmly read a small section of his book. Note that not too much reading was expected of him.

Over time the reading was extended and, as this happened, it was always around about break time—when the child was beginning to get thirsty and the reinforcement (the swing park) was then paired with the drink—that eventually the swing park was phased out.

Only when the problem was ironed out within the home situation was the child slowly weaned back into the classroom.

It was agreed that the child was to be given the class reading assignments a week in advance, so that he had exposure to this material beforehand, which enabled him to deal with any emotional reaction away from the classroom setting.

Therefore the child was better able to integrate into his classroom, and his fellow students did not see the maladaptive behaviour and thus perceive the child as being odd.

Example three

A child from a very superstitious family was born with an extra toe on each of his feet.

On his first excursion, the instructor had taken the child to a play area where there was a sandpit, where the child proceeded to remove his shoes and socks before getting into the sand. As the child did so he scanned the instructor's face for any sign of recognition regarding his toes. Fortunately the instructor had come across this condition before, and was not initially shocked, as he had been when he first encountered a similar situation.

The child then guided the instructor's hand down to his toes. The instructor acknowledged this action by reassuring the child that he was not in any way shocked, doing so by smiling at the child as if there was not the slightest thing wrong. The instructor then took off his own shoes and got into the sand pit with the child and proceeded to sprinkle sand over his own and the child's toes before covering the child's feet and saying: "All gone," followed by "Back again," as the child wriggled his toes free from the sand.

Back in the home environment, the instructor sat with the child and read a book which had been chosen because it portrayed a child who had six toes, as well as creatures with three, four, and sometimes more toes.

As they read the story together the instructor would point out the characters and sometimes count their toes, as well as his own and the child's. This demonstrated to the child that there are many different numbers of toes that one could have—the child in the book had three toes. This was gently pointed out to the child without fuss, as if this were a natural way to read the book.

This method of reading and drawing attention to the characters within the book was extended to other books to maintain this natural way of reading (the first book was not being singled out for specific treatment, thus showing it, or the child, to be different in any way).

In their play time together, the child would have an array of little people figures, and a large caterpillar, which the child would place a figure alongside. The child would then resume playing with the other figures and from time to time would glance at the little figure leaning against the caterpillar.

In an effort to move the child forward, the instructor took a superhero character that the child often played with, and pretended that the superhero was flying to where the little character was beside the caterpillar. Mimicking the superhero, the instructor said: "I'll save you," and lifted the little figure from beside the caterpillar and placed it with all the other little figures. The child looked on without saying or doing anything.

Art work was used to work through the emotions and within a few weeks the child, who had originally refused to take his socks off, was no longer preoccupied with his toes, seemed uninhibited in showing them off, and never again brought the caterpillar into his play scenario.

Example four

A child was obsessively touching all the streetlights as he passed them. The instructor decided to engross him in another activity until the streetlights became secondary.

For instance, when the instructor and the child went out the child was put on his bike so that his hands were occupied, and then whenever they approached a streetlight the instructor would distract the child by saying: "Hurry up, I'll race you," or "Ring your bell." When walking, the instructor would race the child to something beyond the streetlights.

Another ploy that was used was to give the child a branch and tell him to run it along the railings, and make as much noise as he could, thereby distracting him from his obsessive behaviour.

Yet another strategy was to produce a reinforcer that the child wanted very much. As the instructor and child walked past the streetlights the instructor was able to show him the reinforcer whenever it looked as though he was about to touch the streetlight. This was enough to keep the child from indulging in the behaviour.

As time went on the child was asked to put his hands in his pockets as they left the house, and the instructor would engross the child in a conversation which forced the child to look away from the streetlights, such as looking at an aeroplane as it went overhead. Over time the child refrained from touching the streetlights without having to be redirected.

Example five

This example shows how a child can be moved out of a negative mindset by means of a story. It is useful to note the characters a child identifies with—it may well be that he identifies with the victim in the story or, perhaps, as shown in example three, the child identifies with a superhero.

This story is a way in which the child can change the ending to produce a desired outcome, or it can enable the child to become the rescuer and by so doing move him out of his perceived victim mode.

A story that is worth telling is one where the child is trapped in some way. The child is then asked: "What do you think might happen now?"

This acts as a way of enabling him to break free, to create an ending of his own choice. You might like to try this using this story:

Once upon a time, there was a child who lived with his family in a hot, hot country. It so happened that this family were made of wax, and so they had to stay indoors throughout the day to avoid being melted by the hot, hot sun.

All day long the child would stare through the slats of the blinds, which protected the family from the sun, and wish that he were outside with everybody else, sharing the sunshine. However, whenever he said he wanted to be free and go outside, his family would say "No, no, stay here with us, it's safe here."

But one day he could stand it no more, and despite what his family said he dashed outside into the hot, hot sun, and lo and behold he melted under the sun's hot rays.

The family could only watch from within the house, and then when it became cool outside they left the house and fashioned the melted wax into the figure of a bird, and the bird then flew up into the sky—and at last the child was free.

BIBLIOGRAPHY

Breasley, Gill. (1997). *Counselling Children with Special Needs.* Oxford: Blackwell Science.

Cooper, J, Heron, T. & Heward, W. (1987). *Applied Behavior Analysis.* OH: Prentice Hall, Inc.

Golombok, S. & Fivush, R. (1994). *Gender Development.* Cambridge University Press.

Gomez, Lavinia. (1998). *An Introduction to Object Relations.* Free Association Books Ltd.

Klein, Melanie. (1997). *Envy and Gratitude, and other works 1946–1963.*

Laing, R.D. (1959). *The Divided Self.* Tavistock Publications Ltd. Reprinted in Penguin Books 1990.

Laing, R.D. (1971). *Self and Others.* London: Penguin Books Ltd.

Mackintosh, N.J. (1983). *Conditioning & Associative Learning.* Oxford Psychology Series 3. Oxford: Clarendon Press.

Smith, Susan C. (1995). *Interventions with Bereaved Children.* London: Jessica Kingsley Publications.

Sunderland, Margot. (2000). *Using Storytelling as a Therapeutic Tool with Children.* Bicester: Winslow, 2000.

Thurburn, G. (1955). *Voice And Speech.* London: James Nisbet And Co. Ltd.

Wallerstein, Robert S., M.D. (1995). *The Talking Cures.* New Haven, CT: Yale University Press.

Walsh, Graham. (1996). *The Voice of The Child.* (Ed. Ronald Davie). London: Routledge Falmer.

Dott; Home Office. DfEE. (1999). *Working Together to Safeguard Children.* London: The Stationery Office.

Understanding Children's Mental Health. Video produced by Mental Health Media, London.

INDEX

For Product Safety Concerns and Information please contact our EU
representative GPSR@taylorandfrancis.com Taylor & Francis Verlag GmbH,
Kaufingerstraße 24, 80331 München, Germany

Printed and bound by CPI Group (UK) Ltd, Croydon, CR0 4YY
11/04/2025
01843989-0008